START
INVESTING
ONLINE
TODAY!

START
INVESTING
ONLINE
TODAY!

- - Deborah Price - - - - - - - - - -

Adams Media Corporation
Holbrook, Massachusetts

Published by
Adams Media Corporation
260 Center Street, Holbrook, MA 02343. U.S.A.

ISBN: 1-58062-270-4

Printed in the United States of America.

J I H G F E D C B A

Library of Congress Cataloging-in-Publication Data
Price, Deborah.
Start investing online today! / by Deborah Price.
p.   cm.
Includes index.
ISBN 1-58062-270-4
1. Investments--Computer network resources.
2. Portfolio management. I. Title.
HG4515.95. p75   2000
025.06'3326--dc21   99-056504
CIP

This book is available at quantity discounts for bulk purchases.
For information, call 1-800-872-5627.

Visit our exciting small business Web site: www.businesstown.com

AUTHOR'S
Disclaimer

Start Investing Online Today! is written with the intention of providing helpful information regarding online investing. No where is it implied that using the information presented in this book offers any guarantee whatsoever. The author accepts no responsibility or liability for the use or suitability of this material by any person reading this book. The author specifically disclaims any responsibility for any risk or loss (financial or otherwise), associated with, claimed or incurred by the use or application of the contents of this publication. Readers are cautioned and advised to seek the advice of a professional financial advisor or certified public accountant for specific questions and further understanding of the applications of this material and its implications on their personal financial circumstances.

*This book is dedicated to my daughter, Anjelica Price-Rocha,
and her grandmother, Patricia Price.*

Contents

Acknowledgments

A heartfelt thanks to my agent, Sheree Bykofsky, for opening this door. Thanks to my editor, Jere Calmes, at Adams Media for his help and friendship along the way. May thanks to Eric Bolt, (a.k.a., Mr. Asterisk) for everything he did to assist me with this book. Thanks to Lenny Steiner for his wit and wisdom.

A special thanks to Jack Waymire, President and CEO of SAI Financial Advisors, for writing the Foreword to this book.

Thank you, friends and family, for your love and encouragement. I am grateful and blessed to have such wonderful people in my life.

Foreword

Technology is revolutionizing the financial services industry in ways that could not have been imagined just a few short years ago. Every financial firm and advisor in the industry will be impacted by revolutionary changes that are the result of technological innovation. The dividing line between those firms and advisors who will flourish and those who will perish as a result of this innovation is very thin and will be based on their ability to blend their services with new technologies.

One of the primary questions being asked by many industry strategists is whether or not technology will replace professional advisors for the vast majority of investor assets. Will Web-based information and services be so accessible, so easy to use, and of sufficient quality, most investors will feel comfortable making their own financial decisions?

I think investors with substantial assets will continue to utilize personal advisors because managing their own money can be an intimidating, time consuming process. However, I would never underestimate the power of the Internet and the thousands of individuals and companies that are spending billions of dollars to exploit its access to hundreds of millions of global investors.

Many of these investors have the time, knowledge, resources and interest to conduct their own analysis and make their own financial decisions. They are currently the primary customers of the Web-based service companies, including online investing. The number of electronic providers that service these investors will expand exponentially as more and more Websites are developed using increasingly sophisticated software and simulations.

Some of these investors are achieving relatively competitive returns on their assets. And a small percentage is even performing as well as many professionals. However, a growing number of individuals are investing their assets using naive strategies that don't work.

The abnormally high rates of return of the past few years have caused many of them to conclude that managing their own assets is an easy, one step process. For example, buy Cisco Systems and hold it forever. Or, if you are a younger investor with a higher tolerance for risk, buy several Internet stocks issued by technology companies. Why pay a fee or substantial commission for one time advice?

However, an even larger number of investors will continue to use the services of advisors for several reasons. First, they believe professionals can achieve a higher net return than they can on their own. Second, they do not have the knowledge or experience to make unassisted investment decisions. Third, they don't have the time. They are too busy making money or enjoying their money to take the time to invest it. And fourth, they don't like investing their own money.

Another important reason could involve the psychology of investing. A significant percentage of investors like the personal touch, that is, someone who understands them as people. This understanding is both intellectual and emotional. For example, a Website can process information about the intellectual needs of investors, but only another person can truly understand the emotional bases for many of their financial decisions.

Technology is already redefining the role of the financial advisor. The successful advisors of the future will use a blend of technology, advice, value-added services and relationship management. They will provide a number of financial services to investors who are willing to pay for their advice with fees or commissions.

Therein lies one of the biggest challenges facing the financial services industry: The professionals who are going to survive the challenges presented by the online services will have to evolve into "true" advisors who share many of the following characteristics:

They always place the client's interests ahead of their own.

They have the necessary skills to help clients solve financial problems and achieve their financial goals.

They are able to add value by delivering competitive returns on client assets.

They have the skills to help clients manage portfolio risk.

They have strong relationship management skills that enable them to know and understand their clients and their financial circumstances.

Their primary method of compensation is a fee.

It will be impossible for advisors to compete with the online investment services without these characteristics. They cannot compete with information, product sales, and trade executions and expect to win. The online services have tremendous advantages when it comes to cost, accessibility, service menu, technical information, and process.

Advisors and their firms will also have to contend with additional challenges. The quantity of advisors is increasing at the fastest rate in history. Industry veterans are now facing an onslaught of new competition from banks, CPAs, attorneys, and others who are entering the financial advisory marketplace for the first time. Combine this with the thousands of new financial websites and re-engineered wirehouses, and it is clear the pressures facing current firms and advisors are enormous.

The rapidly rising numbers of new financial service providers coupled with a declining supply of investors willing to pay for financial advice is a formula for disaster. And, I believe, many advisors and their firms are choosing to ignore these converging forces. Jungle rules and survival of the fittest will be the new culture for companies and advisors who provide personal financial services. There will no longer be enough business to go around.

Advisors have their challenges, but so do the electronic providers. For example, Websites will have to deliver user-friendly information that helps investors make informed, high-quality financial decisions. This won't be an easy task, because online services will never "know" the client as well as an advisor.

The ultimate winners will be the advisors and Websites that most effectively blend quality advice, value-added services and state-of-the-art technology into one convenient platform. The challenge for the Websites will be to offer electronic services with an effective process for making investment decisions. The challenge for advisors will be to weave technology into their services in a way that maintains their clients' dependency on them for advice.

In the future, investors will have distinct choices for how they manage their assets, although the choices may blur over time. Online services, personal advisors or a blend of the two—the future will be much different than the past.

Jack Waymire
President & CEO
SAI Financial Advisors

Introduction: Online Investing— The New Frontier

In the past year I have been asked by friends, clients, and complete strangers to *please* help them learn how to trade online. Everyone it seems has caught online trading fever, and it wasn't long before I found myself feeling sympathetic and agreeing to assist people. As a financial advisor I have always considered myself first and foremost a teacher and skillful handholder. In particular, the hands of nervous investors who fear that pressing the wrong button on the computer screen could possibly cause their portfolio to float off in cyberspace, lost forever.

I wrote this book for two reasons. One, I want potential online investors to know that money does not just disappear because you accidentally push the wrong button or your computer crashes while viewing your portfolio online. Money disappears by making bad investment decisions. The potential for making bad investment decisions increases when you are uninformed, unprepared, or undisciplined.

The second reason I wrote this book was to help educate and prepare those who have the desire to invest online. This book is a primer intended to facilitate and encourage people who have decided to take this step. It will provide you with the basics of what you need to get started. If you desire to learn more, there is no shortage of information to help with your continuing education. Knowledge needs to increase in steps, especially where your hard-earned money is concerned. Just because technology has the ability to fast-forward our lives doesn't mean we should all allow it. This is one of those situations where you might want to hit the pause button on the remote control. Try not to press play or fast forward unless you're really ready.

Online investing has become the new frontier that everyone wants to explore. It is the hot topic of conversation that is leading millions of people from traditional off-line investing to investing on the Internet. The allure and novelty of online investing is also creating an entirely new population of investors. Suddenly, people who have never invested at all are investing online or considering it, as you are.

While online investing is gaining momentum rapidly, it remains to be seen how the average online investor will fare in comparison to those who are sticking with their advisors and brokers off-line. Following an 11 percent drop off the high of the market as of October 1999, we witnessed a significant decrease in the interest and popularity of daytrading. There is nothing quite like a market correction to weed out the investors from the speculators. More people are beginning to realize that market speculation is a financially dangerous game. You might as well go to Las Vegas and place a chip on red or black in a game of roulette. The only difference is in Las Vegas you get free drinks, a room and a show. The stock market is not that generous; when you lose, you just lose. There is nothing entertaining or glamorous about it. If you're interested in gambling with your money or being a daytrader, this is not the book for you.

This book was written for people who want to become wise investors. *Start Investing Online Today* is written in a step-by-step format, similar to the way an Investing 101 class would be taught. As the author of this book, I have no idea where you, the reader, may be in your investment learning curve. If you already have some background and experience, you could easily skip ahead and begin online investing sooner than this book directs you. However, if you're a novice investor, you are more likely to be a successful investor if you follow the book's guidelines from beginning to end.

Investing online is a great and exciting opportunity, but it should be approached in an educated manner. Whether you're investing online or off, sound investment principles should be used along with a game plan. The greatest potential threat to online investors is not what they know, but what they don't know. Take the time to know. Avoid the temptation to rush in and make financial decisions that could be costly. It takes years to accumulate money and only seconds to lose it by being impulsive. If at any point in this book you get stuck and feel uncertain how to proceed, consider hiring an expert. There is no reason why you can't go online, trade for your own account, and have an advisor to guide you as well. Over time as you gain more knowledge and confidence, you can always go it alone.

Investors had difficulty enough with financial decisions before online investing became an option. The more options we have, the more difficult it becomes to make wise investment choices. Hopefully, this book will serve as the bridge to greater understanding. It is wonderful that online investing has created a venue for more people to become investors. However, online investing will only serve us as investors if we approach this new frontier intelligently and responsibly. It is in all our interests to maintain a reasonably safe and sane investment marketplace in which we all may prosper. I wish you great success as you embark on your online investing adventure.

PART ONE

BECOMING

AN

ONLINE

PIONEER

C H A P T E R   O N E

Preparing for the Trip

I think the necessity of being ready increases.
Look to it.

—ABRAHAM LINCOLN, 1861

We are and always will be a country of pioneers. It is part of our heritage to constantly seek new frontiers. Online trading is the new frontier where fortunes can be made or lost in nanoseconds. Unlike our ancestors, the pioneers of today can sit back in the comfort of their home, in an ergonomically correct chair, and search the entire world for investment opportunities via the Internet.

Today, in the largest global marketplace ever imagined, we can buy, sell, and trade both goods and investments twenty-four hours a day with electronic currency and the click of a mouse. Without question, online trading offers tremendous opportunities for both the financial world and individual investors that have not previously existed. However, this new frontier remains uncharted territory and should be approached carefully and with proper due diligence. Whether you trade online or off, a successful investment strategy requires time, consideration, and knowledge. A wise investor doesn't abandon sound investment advice simply because the availability and options for participating have become more accessible.

Without question, anyone who has the time, willingness, and desire to be an online investor can learn how to invest his or her own money. However, it should be said up front that online trading is not for everyone. It is not for the faint of heart or the financially fearful. If you are the type of person who has always invested in CDs (certificates of deposit) and worry constantly about where to put your money when your next CD matures, you should approach online investing cautiously. In fact, no matter what your history of investing is, if you already live with a great deal of financial fear, online investing will not ease your anxiety. It is essential that you become familiar with the road ahead of you and take the necessary steps to ensure your preparedness before you begin to trade online.

Preparing for the Trip

Two of the most important things you will need to evaluate before you begin online trading are the type of investor you are and your investor profile. You will need to understand and develop the skills and characteristics necessary to becoming a successful online pioneer. All investors are not alike, nor should they be. Every individual has his or her own particular needs, financial goals, and objectives, not to mention risk tolerance. It is critical that you understand your needs and decide what investments and strategies are appropriate for you.

Time Out

There is never going to be one financial plan, investment, or strategy that is right for everyone. Each person needs to evaluate a variety of factors, such as age, income needs, dependents, personality profile, and risk tolerance before choosing any investment.

Most people need help and guidance in learning how to develop a financial plan and investment strategy. This book will provide a roadmap to assist you in assessing your financial profile and give you a clear understanding of what you need to know before you get started. It will also help you decide if online investing is right for you and if so, how to proceed in a manner that is prudent and appropriate for you.

Unlike the early pioneers, you can take a trip around the online trading world without the risk of losing your life, that is, unless you suffer a heart attack one day while watching the market head south and seeing your net worth drop in half. (Don't laugh, it can happen.) If you want to be an online investor, you should be prepared to become an educated investor. You'll need to learn how to weed out "good" investments from the "bad" in a world that is filled with unscrupulous fortune hunters.

We are fortunate to have governmental and outside agencies dedicated to serving and protecting the investing public. The Securities and Exchange Commission (SEC), a governmental agency, and the National Association of Securities Dealers (NASD), a securities-industry organization, are the primary agencies responsible for regulating the investment industry and the stock market exchanges. However, even they can only do so much. New rules and regulations are currently being introduced into legislation to help squelch online investment scams. In the meantime, online scams continue to proliferate and have become more sophisticated than ever before.

Understanding the Territory

Go To

Tips to help avoid such scams will be handled in detail in Chapter 11 of this book.

As an online investor, it is important that you understand the nature and territory of this ever changing, fast moving marketplace. According to recent figures, there are approximately 30 million American households using the Internet (source: *Forbes*, October 1998). Of those 30 million, almost 6 million people currently trade online and that number is growing rapidly. The stampede to online trading has definitely begun. In the first quarter of 1999, the total average online trading volume was approximately 444,000 trades per day. That represents more than a 363 percent increase in volume since the first quarter of 1997, when the average trading volume was approximately 95,000 trades per day (source: Credit Suisse First Boston Corporation).

Bumps in the Road

In the period from October of 1997 to April of 1999, over 3,000 complaints were received by the SEC regarding problems associated with online trading. That represents an increase in complaints of more than 500 percent from the previous period (from October 1996 to October 1997), during which time only 259 complaints were filed. It is obvious by looking at these figures that the online trading business still has a way to go before they perfect their technology and operations. (Which is all the more reason to become as educated as possible before entering this market.)

Rapid Rise in Trading Problems

In 1998, a record number of more than 53,000 complaints and inquiries were handled by the SEC (Securities and Exchange Commission). It is interesting to note however, that while complaints against individual brokers have actually dropped, the number of complaints launched against invest-ment companies (referred to as broker/dealers) has risen dramatically. The types of complaints range from operational problems, delays in account transfers, and errors in processing orders to delays or failures to properly execute orders. The ten most common complaints received by the SEC are as follows:

Type of complaint	1997	1998	% Increase/Decrease
Misrepresentations in selling a product	1,324	1,232	- 7%
Transfer of account problems	834	1,180	+41%
Unauthorized transactions	1,338	1,124	- 16%
Failure to follow an investor's instructions	992	830	- 16%
Concern about the way a corporation conducts its ordinary business	532	763	+43%
Failure to process or delays in executing orders	470	721	+53%
Problems about 401(k) plans or pension plans	378	702	+86%
Failure to distribute money to investors	611	605	- 1%
Errors in processing orders	261	594	+127%
Failure to send securities certificates to investors	592	587	- 1%

(Source: SEC Web site, www.sec.gov)

With respect to online trading complaints specifically, the three most common complaints have been:

1. Difficulties in accessing accounts.
2. Delays or failures in the execution of orders.
3. Errors in processing orders.

(Source: SEC Web site)

This book will provide you with tips and strategies that can greatly help reduce these risks. It should be noted however, that the unprepared and uneducated investor is far more likely to encounter online trading problems than one who has dedicated time and energy to developing his or her skills.

Assessing Your Readiness

Before you proceed, consider how prepared you actually are to begin trading online. The following questionnaire will help assess your readiness to become on online pioneer. It should also serve as a guideline when considering how much time, energy, and money you are willing to commit to your initial online education.

On a separate piece of paper number 1–20. Indicate an A for answers that strongly apply to you, S for answers that somewhat apply to you, and N for answers that never apply to you.

1. I have one or more brokerage accounts that have been open for one year or longer.
2. I am already an active investor who has been investing for one year or longer.
3. I have been interested in investing and the financial world for one year or longer.
4. I have savings that are currently not invested and can afford to take some risk in investing some of this money.
5. I have a secure job or a regular source of income.
6. I am not concerned about needing to tap into my invested assets anytime in the near future.

7. I have time to dedicate to learning about investment products and investment strategies.
8. I am familiar with different types of investments.
9. I have a working knowledge of investment terminology.
10. I enjoy reading financial newspapers and publications.
11. I have a lot of self-discipline and can easily teach myself anything I am interested in.
12. I enjoy conducting independent research regarding various types of investing.
13. I own my own computer and use it regularly.
14. I enjoy working with computers and have no fear or resistance to becoming a knowledgeable online investor.
15. I am familiar with the Internet and surf the web on a regular basis.
16. I consider myself to be financially responsible and not prone to taking unnecessary risk.
17. If I have a plan, I can easily stick to it regardless of the outside influence or market circumstances.
18. I am not prone to making impulsive decisions without having all the facts.
19. I am interested in being a long-term investor who invests in a manner that is appropriate to my personal and financial needs.
20. I do not consider online investing an opportunity to get rich quickly but rather an educated investment choice to be actively involved in creating my own financial destiny.

Key to Assessment Questionnaire

If you have fifteen or more A responses, you are fairly well prepared to become an online investor. This book will be easy for you to assimilate and act on quickly.

A score of ten or more S answers indicate that you have some knowledge and the willingness and desire to learn more.

Every S or N response is a specific area of knowledge that you need to pay attention to and become more educated on.

Ten or more N responses is a strong sign that you need to read every page of this book word for word or you're likely to get in over your head and risk losing money quickly. Depending on your learning curve, time, and objectives, you may want to consider working with a professional investment advisor who is willing to help educate you and give you individual guidance before you try this on your own.

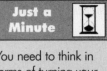

Just a Minute

You need to think in terms of turning your S and N answers into A answers. This book will help you achieve that in a step-by-step process.

Guidelines for Success

Go To

The lesson in Chapter 7 will cover the pros and cons of working with or without professional guidance.

Why is it so important to have all, or most of, the previous questionnaire's statements apply to you affirmatively? In going down the list starting with number one, for example, if you do not already have a brokerage or investment account and some minimal investment experience, you need to acquire some background on the basics of investing. In Chapter 3 you will learn basic investing, which will provide an overview of investments by type, definition, and their primary objective.

As you begin to clarify the areas you need to work on in order to be a successful online investor, you'll know which chapters and subjects to devote more attention to. For example, if you have never had an investment account or do not presently own any securities, you'll find help on how to open an account and account types in Chapter 8. If you have not actively traded securities, Chapter 12 will help you to develop knowledge about how the stock market works and how to execute orders properly. One of the crucial challenges to being an online investor is taking an active interest in the financial world and developing skills to help you understand how the financial markets work.

Know Your Financial Limits

In regard to the savings and assets you have, it is essential that you know the difference between liquid savings and investable assets. It is not prudent to have all your money invested. How much money you need to keep in reserve (i.e. in liquid savings or money market accounts) varies from one individual to the next. If you have a secure job and income flow, you can probably afford to invest more than someone whose income is not stable or comes in erratically from month to month.

Time Out

The surest way to lose money is to invest money that you find yourself needing because of an unexpected cash flow problem, forcing you to sell an investment at a loss.

You should never invest money that you can't afford to lose. You cannot blame an investment for losing money if you are forced to sell it before it has time to perform. That is simply an example of a poor investment strategy. Investments do not always make money quickly. Almost any investment can drop in value immediately after you purchase it due to bad news or market circumstances. A drop in value is not necessarily an indication that something is wrong with that investment. Investments, particularly individual stocks and stock mutual funds, need time to grow. Smart investors know that investing is not about timing the market. It's about *time in the market*. It's your choice, but be aware that most investors lose money because they sell their investments too soon. They make an investment, it drops in value or the market corrects, and they get fearful and sell. Buying and selling investments impulsively or on emotion is not an investment strategy, it's financial suicide. Quite literally, buying and selling in this manner will kill any investment opportunity you might have had. It will also create a tremendous amount of stress and anxiety in your life.

Occasionally a client will call me with the sound of panic in his voice and say, "I just got my statement and I can't believe how much XYZ stock has dropped." While the client is talking, I'll have pulled the most current news and research on XYZ stock and, nine times out of ten, there is nothing fundamentally wrong with the stock. Within about two minutes I can tell the client why the stock dropped and why he shouldn't worry about it. My response is based upon the available facts at the moment, not an emotional reaction.

Develop Your Confidence

It takes a long time to become confident in your ability to make good financial decisions and investment choices. I have been investing money for clients for almost fifteen years, and I can honestly tell you that the first couple of years were nerve-wracking. I could not go on vacation or take a day off without constantly worrying about the market and how my clients' money was doing. Even though I believed that I had made good investment choices, I lacked the confidence and experience to know for certain.

Time Saver

Learning to conduct quick fact-finding missions and making unemotional financial decisions is one of the most important skills you need to learn to be an online investor.

On October 19, 1987, I experienced my first real taste of my ability. I will never forget it. Black Monday was one of the most stressful experiences of my life. I was powerless to do anything to stop the market from spiraling downward (as any investor—professional, or otherwise—always is). The only thing I could do was tell my clients to fasten their seat belts and hold on. I urged all of them to simply hold their positions. Only two clients insisted on selling. Those are the only two clients who took actual losses on their portfolio. Clients who suffered paper losses recovered from the crash and were profitable again within sixteen months or less. It was the greatest lesson I could ever learn. It proved to me that I had done my homework. My advice and investment choices for my clients survived and continued to thrive in the years that followed. I was also given the opportunity to develop the seeds of confidence that have continued to grow over the years, giving me a comfort level that I hope this book helps others to attain.

Time Out

A crash or significant correction can be your greatest teacher if you're prepared. It can be your biggest nightmare if you're not.

Throughout this book you will learn the most important elements of creating an investment plan that you can live with in any market cycle. By the time you've finished this book you'll be a more educated and confident investor, and you will be ready to place your first online trade.

CHAPTER TWO

Charting Your Course

Knowledge advances by steps, and not by leaps.

—LORD MACAULAY

The average American will earn over one million dollars in his lifetime and save less than 10 percent of it. As a result, one of the greatest financial concerns facing Americans today is not when they will retire but how. The U.S. government has publicly defined this situation as a financial crisis. In an effort to increase public awareness, the government has established a financial literacy program dedicated to providing information and education about the importance of saving and investing.

One of the main reasons that people fail to accomplish their personal and financial goals is a lack of planning. Many studies clearly indicate the importance of writing down your goals and mapping out a plan for achieving them. A Harvard University study concluded that almost all of the students who took the time to write down their goals accomplished them. Students participating in the study who did not write down their goals accomplished far less in comparison.

It is amazing to think that we spend most of our adult lives working to make money (an average of over 1,800 hours per year), yet spend relatively few hours planning how to invest that money wisely. Perhaps the fascination with the Internet and its relative ease and convenience will change this situation. Conceivably, the novelty and excitement inspired by online trading will become a venue for getting more people involved in saving, investing, and planning for their future. If so, it will have served a great purpose. However, online investing should not be approached like a trip to Las Vegas. So before you begin investing on the Internet, here are a few key steps to follow to increase the odds of your financial success.

Key Steps to Follow

CREATE A WRITTEN FINANCIAL PLAN

Make sure you have a financial plan and investment strategy that is suitable for you and that you write it down. Although it's great to share information with others, what is appropriate for your next door neighbor may be entirely inappropriate for you. Creating a plan will help you develop specific goals and objectives that are in line with your financial needs and concerns, both now and in the future.

RESEARCH, RESEARCH, RESEARCH

When you conduct your own research with the use of reliable sources, you will be able to make educated buying and selling decisions. There are over 8,000 mutual funds to choose from and more than 15,000 stock issues. If you don't perform adequate research, you might as well throw darts at the business section and get used to losing money.

SELECT APPROPRIATE INVESTMENTS

Once you've developed a plan and conducted your research, you'll be ready to make some educated investment decisions. Your plan will help you determine what kind of investments are most suitable to achieve your financial goals in the time horizon you need to meet them.

Key point: The more time you have, the more risk you can afford to take. If you're thirty years old, you have time to make some mistakes and

take some losses. That is not to say you should ever be taking any unnecessary risk but that in general younger people simply have more time to
recover and learn their lesson, so to speak. If you are fifty or older, you
don't have time to recover from investing too speculatively. Actually, the
only thing that will ensure protection from the volatility of today's market
is time and diversification. No one should ever put all his or her eggs in
one basket. You need a plan that has several baskets, with different kinds
of investments in each.

Diversify Your Assets

Due to the vast number of available choices, you will need to develop
a firm list of criteria for how to select specific investments. These criteria
should be based on your comfort zone and should mirror the goals established in your financial plan. For example, one way to pick a mutual fund
is to only evaluate mutual funds that have a track record of ten years or
more (or funds that are managed by portfolio managers with at least a
ten-year history of managing money.) That elimi-
nates a lot of funds, but it will provide you with
the funds that have the longest track record. This
is simply one method of screening an investment.
It may not be the one for you.

Determine Your Investment Time Horizon

The proper way to measure the quality of an
investment is not how well it performed in the last
year or even three years, but how well it has performed in the long run. This is a key point to
remember when developing your plan. What
exactly is your time horizon for investing? How
long do you need to have your money growing
for you? Or, if you're an income investor, how
long do you anticipate needing an income from
your investments?

Keep in mind that we have been riding the
fastest, longest bull market in history. The returns
on investments in recent years are unprecedented.

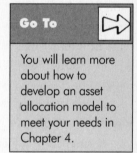

Go To

You will learn more
about how to
develop an asset
allocation model to
meet your needs in
Chapter 4.

Just a Minute

The longer your time
horizon is, the more
concerned you
should be about
looking at the track
record and historical
performance of the
investments you're
selecting.

Any investor expecting these exceptionally high returns to continue indefinitely is setting himself up for disappointment. Your criteria should be realistic and allow you to feel like you've succeeded. This can be achieved when your expectations are in line with the historical performance of the market and not the anomaly of recent returns.

DEVELOP A STRATEGY

Once you have prepared a plan, conducted your due diligence and research, developed your criteria for investing, and made your investment selections, you will need to adopt an investment strategy and then *stick to it.*

This book will teach you not only how to become an online investor, it will teach you to become a wise investor. Let's face it, anybody can push a button and trade securities. Not everyone who does so makes money or sleeps well at night. That should be your primary goal. If you work toward that end, you will not have read this book and done all this work for nothing. You will be prepared and armed with all the right skills and tools to build your financial future. However, you will need to develop the discipline to maintain your strategy. Just because the market goes down, you should not necessarily alter your plan. Unless there are significant changes in the fundamentals of a particular investment that are more than temporary setbacks, you should maintain your strategy. If you have done your homework, you can be confident in your decisions. It is essential that you learn to separate your investments from your emotions. Throughout this book you will be given tips and strategies to acquire this greatly needed skill.

Time Out

To be an online pioneer you must become an investor who makes sound financial decisions based upon fact rather than emotional reaction.

LEARN THE LANGUAGE

In becoming an online investor you will also need to become familiar with market patterns, terminology, trading practices, rules, and regulations. For example, did you know that you could be convicted of insider trading if you knowingly use information that is not publicly available for personal gain? That means this: If your brother-in-law tells you that his company is about to announce a recent technological development that is not yet public information and you proceed to tell all your friends and relatives to go out and buy this hot stock, you would have violated a federal securities law (as did your brother-in-law and everyone else who used the information and traded the XYZ stock). This is a punishable offense.

KNOW THE LAWS

Insider trading laws have been expanded in recent years to include virtually anybody as being potentially liable for use of nonpublic information. Although your personal liability managing your own investments is far less than that of a professional offering advice to the public, you are not granted immunity for failure to comply with certain rules and regulations. That goes for other laws as well.

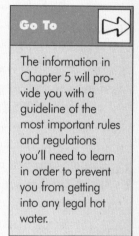

Go To

The information in Chapter 5 will provide you with a guideline of the most important rules and regulations you'll need to learn in order to prevent you from getting into any legal hot water.

KNOW YOURSELF

If you were a licensed professional investment advisor, you would be required by law to conform to a securities regulation known as Rule 405, Know Your Customer. The essence of this regulation is that *before* a client's money is invested, investment professionals are legally obligated to get to know their customer's needs and investor profile. If you ultimately decide to work with a professional, they should go through this process with you in the early stages of your relationship. Regardless of whether you choose to work with a professional or not, it is absolutely essential that you apply Rule 405 and Know Yourself before you begin online trading. No, you aren't legally obligated, but completing this process is in your own best interest and will provide a framework from which to begin investing.

By now you have had a chance to evaluate the course ahead. Based upon your responses to the questionnaire provided in Chapter 1, you have also had the opportunity to see the areas you need to pay particular attention to as you proceed with your education. But before you get started, let's take a look at your investor profile and help you decide what kind of investor you are or hope to be.

Investor Profile Quiz

1. Which of the following reasons do you need to save and invest your money? (Check all that apply)
   - a) Buy a home
   - b) Buy a car
   - c) Fund a child's education
   - ◄ d) Start a business
   - ◄ e) Have a comfortable retirement
   - f) Provide for the long-term care of a dependent or elderly parent

2. How soon will you be needing money for any one of the reason that you checked above? (Indicate your time horizon next to each item that you checked above)

3. If you lost your job or became too sick to work, how long could you live off your liquid savings before having to dip into your investment assets?

4. As an investor, what percentage of your investable dollars would you feel comfortable investing in individual stocks?
   - a) 75% or greater
   - b) up to 50%
   - c) up to 25%
   - d) 10% or less

5. How much would you feel comfortable investing in mutual funds?
   - a) 75% or greater
   - b) up to 50%
   - c) up to 25%
   - d) 10% or less

6. How much would you feel comfortable investing in government, corporate, or municipal bonds?
   - a) 10% or less
   - b) up to 25%
   - c) up to 50%
   - d) 75% or greater

7. How much of your income, if any, are you depending on your investments to provide for you?
    — a) I am not depending on my investments for income.
    b) approximately 50% of my income
    c) all of my income
8. What are your primary investment objectives?
    a) aggressive growth
    — b) growth
    c) growth and income
    d) income
9. Which statement most closely reflects your ability to tolerate market volatility?
    a) I consider myself a long-term investor and I am willing to take considerable risk as long as my overall returns are favorable.
    — b) I feel comfortable with some amount of risk as long as my money is invested in a diversified portfolio of high-quality investments with a proven track record.
    c) I feel very uncomfortable with market volatility and would rather have a lower return on my portfolio than risk losing.
10. How concerned are you overall about the preservation of principal of your invested assets?
    a) not concerned
    — b) somewhat concerned
    c) very concerned
11. What percentage drop in principal do you feel you could tolerate before becoming very anxious, prompting you to liquidate all or part of your portfolio?
    a) I could handle a drop of 50%
    b) I could handle a drop of up to 25%
    — c) I could handle a drop of up to 10%
    d) I could not handle any drop in principal
12. Which of the following statements is the most accurate about your risk tolerance and investment objectives?
    a) I want my investments to grow significantly over time and I do not anticipate needing my investments for income for at least ten years.

➤ b) I need my investments to grow over time, but I will be needing income within about five years.

c) I need my investment to grow, but I also need current income.

d) My primary concern is income and safety of principal.

13. What do you consider a good return on your investments?

➤ a) 15% or more

b) 10 to 12%

c) 8 to 10%

d) 5 to 7%

14. How much experience and comfort do you have working with computers?

a) I am highly experienced and feel very comfortable.

➤ b) I have some experience and I'm willing to commit time to learning and becoming more comfortable.

c) I have little or no experience and I'm relatively uncomfortable using computers at this time.

15. How much experience do you have using the Internet?

a) I am very experienced and use the Internet frequently.

➤ b) I have some experience but need to learn more.

c) I have little or no experience.

16. How much time do you currently spend reading investment or financial books and publications?

➤ a) I read financial newspapers and publications daily.

b) I read financial newspapers and publications occasionally.

c) I seldom read financial newspapers or publications.

17. In general, how knowledgeable do you consider yourself regarding investment and financial matters?

a) I am considerably knowledgeable.

➤ b) I am somewhat knowledgeable.

c) I have very little knowledge.

18. How much time do you have that you are willing to commit to becoming a savvy online investor?

➤ a) Whatever it takes.

b) I'm willing to dedicate an hour a day.

c) I have very little available time to commit.

To determine your investor profile, add up the number of a, b, c , and d answers you have.

Give yourself 4 points for every a answer.
Give yourself 3 points for every b answer.
Give yourself 2 points for every c answer.
Give yourself 1 point for every d answer.

For questions one and two subtract one point for every financial need you have that has a time horizon of three years or less.

For question three, subtract another point if you have less than one year's protection in the event of a job loss or illness.

A score of 50 points or more indicates that you have an aggressive investor profile and can take more risk than the average investor. You probably expect a high rate of return on your investments and are willing to accept a high degree of risk to accomplish your financial goals. You are likely to become (or may already be) an online t-radar. You are an excellent candidate for on-line trading and will probably be a successful pioneer. However, you must be careful not to be overly speculative.

A score of 35 to 40 points indicates that you have a moderate to aggressive investor profile. You are willing to accept some risk but will probably be more methodical in your strategy and not trade as actively as the more aggressive investor. You are likely more suited to investing most of your money in high quality versus speculative investments. You are also a good online investment candidate.

A score of 25 to 35 points indicates that you have the profile of a moderate investor. You are not likely to be comfortable trading securities frequently and will more than likely adopt a "buy and hold" approach to investing. You have the ability to be a good online investor but will need to make certain that you take an active role in maintaining your strategy and do not become complacent.

A score of 15 to 25 points is a good indication that you are a more conservative investor and are more concerned with preservation of principal than the growth of your portfolio. Although you are willing to take some risk, it is unlikely that you would be comfortable "risking" many of your investable dollars. You should approach online investing with a great deal of caution, since it is not a place you would easily feel comfortable. You might consider working with a professional before you go it alone.

A score of 5 to 15 indicates that you have an ultra-conservative investor profile and have little or no risk tolerance. You would probably be more comfortable sleeping on your money under your mattress than risk losing any principal in the market. You are not a good candidate for becoming an online trader, but if you insist on trying, take a small amount of money and be prepared to lose money and sleep.

Time Out

Remember, as I stated early in this chapter, online investing is not for everyone. In this case, that would include ultra-conservative investors.

The following chapter will go into greater detail about the various risks and rewards that are associated with investing in each type of investment that can be traded online. It will also provide you with a guideline for investing in specific investments based upon your investor profile.

CHAPTER THREE

Planning Your Strategy

Festina lente. (Make haste slowly.)

—AUGUSTUS, 63 B.C.

It is now time to learn how to create a financial plan based upon your investor profile and risk tolerance. By the end of this chapter you will have clearly defined what your goals and objectives are and will be armed with a game plan that will serve as the road map to your financial future.

Investing is a very personal experience. Each individual should develop a financial plan based upon goals and objectives that are specific to his or her needs and desires. In other words, a financial plan is really only meaningful to the extent that it helps you achieve what is important to you and that the process of getting there is a reasonably comfortable one. For example, if you were to use the financial plan and investment strategy of your best friend, but his long-term goals and desires were completely different than yours, you would probably feel frustrated and unhappy with the outcome. It's like wearing the clothes of someone who is a different size. It just doesn't fit.

A financial plan is simply an attempt to chart your life's course within the context of your goals and desires. In order to create the life you desire it is important that you make conscious decisions about your finances. Money, when given the proper care and attention, is a resource that can facilitate the direction of your life. The financial plan you create will become the road map for your money and help guide the direction of your life. So before we proceed with how to invest, let's take a close look at why you're investing.

In general, people are more likely to follow through with what they've started when it has personal meaning and value to them. This is true of financial planning as well. To make your plan meaningful and valuable to you, begin by making a list of all the goals and objectives you have for doing this in the first place. Use the following example to assist you.

Ms. Smith, age thirty-five, has a moderate to aggressive investor profile. She currently has $20,000 of which she plans to invest $15,000 online and keep $5,000 in a money market account as an emergency fund. In order of priority, she has listed her goals and objectives within the time frame she hopes to achieve them.

Ms. Smith's goals:

- Save $5,000 to finish master's degree in three years.
- Save $25,000 to buy a house in three years.
- Save $20,000 to start private practice in five years.
- Save $2,000 per year in an IRA.
- Save $3,000 for trip to Europe in four years.
- Save amount necessary to retire comfortably at age sixty.

Ms. Smith's bigger picture objectives as they correspond to each goal:

1. Completing her master's degree will increase her job prospects and income. It is also necessary for licensing so that she can eventually have her own business.
2. She wants to buy a house before she makes any other major financial or career decisions. Owning her own home is very important to her. Also, she plans to create a home office, if possible, on her property. Buying a house will also reduce her

taxes so that she can keep and invest more of the money she makes.

3. She has always wanted to be self-employed and feels that she'll be personally and professionally ready in about five years.

4. She wants to contribute $2,000 a year to an IRA so that she can retire comfortably by the time she's sixty. She does wish to work as long as she possibly can but needs to plan for the possibility that she might need to slow down in her sixties.

5. After she finishes her master's she wants to take a long-deserved break and go to Europe. She has been putting this on the back burner for too long and has now put a priority on it by making it a part of her plan.

Just a Minute

Having an idea of the time frame you need to meet your goals and objectives in is critical to your investment strategy. Knowing when you need to have your investment capital available is important in helping you choose the right investments.

It's clear that Ms. Smith has a lot of things going for her. She knows what she wants, she's done her homework, she's focused, and she has a plan that she's committed to. She's ready to move forward. How about you?

List your goals and objectives in order of priority. Each goal should have an amount of money that is needed (approximate if necessary) and a time horizon. For each goal you have, what is your ultimate objective? Why is it important to you, personally and/or financially, to achieve each of your goals? This is the time to take out your dreams, dust them off, and begin to create a plan to make them happen.

Before you go any further you'll need to do a little homework. Two essential ingredients of a financial plan that help direct your investing is a summary of your income and expenses (yes, that terrible b-word known as "the budget") and a list of your assets and liabilities. You may have already done this and can use or update the information you already have. If this is your first time, all you need to do is fill in the blanks and do the math. Most people gain a lot of financial insight by doing

Time Saver

Remember, there are no right answers, only *your* answers.
This is your financial plan. Frame it so that it fits the picture you envision for your life.

this exercise, so try not to skip over this part. Remember, if you don't know where you stand financially now, how can you expect to know where you're going?

Figure 3-1
Summary of Income & Expenses (fill in the blanks)

Monthly Income Summary

Salary, wages	$ _____
Alimony, child support	$ _____
Interest income	$ _____
Dividend income	$ _____
Social Security benefits	$ _____
Pensions	$ _____
Other income	$ _____

Total Monthly Income $ _____

Monthly expenses

Mortgage, rent	$ _____	Car payment	$ _____
Personal loans	$ _____	Car expenses (gas, etc.)	$ _____
Credit cards	$ _____	Car insurance	$ _____
Tax payments	$ _____	Medical insurance	$ _____
Utilities	$ _____	Disability insurance	$ _____
Food/groceries	$ _____	Unreimbursed healthcare	$ _____
Clothing	$ _____	Entertainment	$ _____
Dry cleaning	$ _____	Vacation/travel	$ _____
Personal (hair, etc.)	$ _____	Dues (clubs, hobbies)	$ _____
Childcare	$ _____	Professional services	$ _____
Education expenses	$ _____	Gifts	$ _____
Miscellaneous expenses	$ _____	Charitable expenses	$ _____

Total Monthly Expenses $ _____

Net Cash Flow

Total monthly income	$ _____
Minus total monthly expenses	$ _____
Equals your bottom line	$ _____
(Discretionary Income)	

Summary of Assets

Cash and Cash Equivalents
Checking accounts $ _____
Savings accounts $ _____
Money market funds $ _____
Certificates of deposit $ _____
Other cash reserves $ _____

Tangible assets
Residence $ _____
Rental Property $ _____
Vacation Home $ _____
Furnishings $ _____
Art, collectibles $ _____

Investment assets
Stocks $ _____
Mutual funds $ _____
Variable annuities $ _____
Fixed annuities $ _____
Limited partnerships $ _____
Trust deeds $ _____
Precious metals $ _____
U.S. Government Bonds $ _____
Treasury Bills $ _____
Corporate Bonds $ _____
Municipal Bonds $ _____

Total Value of Assets $ _____

Liabilities
Residence mortgage $ _____
Other mortgages $ _____
Auto loans $ _____
Bank loans $ _____
Personal loans $ _____
Credit card debt $ _____
Other debts $ _____

Total Liabilities $ _____

Total assets $ _____
Minus total liabilities $ _____
Your Net Worth $ _____

At this point you should be equipped with the following information about yourself:

Your investor profile
Your goals and objectives
Your summary of monthly income and expenses
Your net worth

Now it's time to begin combining these ingredients into a specific financial plan. Do this on your computer now. Log on to the Internet and go to the Web site *http://www.financenter.com*. This site provides many types of financial calculators that will help you create your financial plan. The calculators are simple and easy to use.

Just fill in the blanks as they apply to you. If you don't like this calculator site, turn to the reference section of this book for a list of other sources.

At this Web site, you can choose from a variety of financial calculators that will assist you with this lesson. Here's a list of what's available:

- savings calculator
- education calculator
- investment calculator
- retirement calculator
- mortgage calculator
- credit calculator
- budgeting calculator

Click on the financial calculator that you need to work with, using your list of goals and objectives as a guideline.

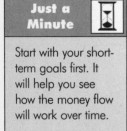

Just a Minute

Start with your short-term goals first. It will help you see how the money flow will work over time.

Before you begin you'll need some guidance regarding what return on your investments to assume and enter into the calculator. Although your actual rate of return on your investments will vary depending upon your investment choices and experience, you need to assume an appropriate return for the purpose of this exercise.

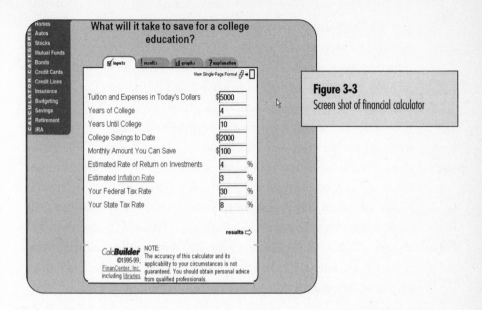

What will it take to save for a college education?

| ☑ inputs | ! results | ⊞ graphs | ? explanation |

View Single-Page Format

Tuition and Expenses in Today's Dollars	$5000	
Years of College	4	
Years Until College	10	
College Savings to Date	$2000	
Monthly Amount You Can Save	$100	
Estimated Rate of Return on Investments	4	%
Estimated Inflation Rate	3	%
Your Federal Tax Rate	30	%
Your State Tax Rate	8	%

results ⇨

Calc**Builder**
©1995-99,
FinanCenter, Inc.
including libraries

NOTE:
The accuracy of this calculator and its applicability to your circumstances is not guaranteed. You should obtain personal advice from qualified professionals.

Figure 3-3
Screen shot of financial calculator

By investor profile, reasonable rates of return that can be assumed for this purpose are as follows:

Aggressive—12% or higher
Aggressive to Moderate—10 to 12%
Moderate—8 to 10%
Moderate to Conservative—6 to 8%
Conservative—5 to 7%
Ultraconservative—2 to 5%

Choose a rate of return that is in line with your risk tolerance and investor profile. If you're uncertain, go back to the questionnaire in Chapter 2 and make sure you've answered the questions honestly.

Using Ms. Smith as our example, this is how her financial plan turned out after inputting her financial information into the calculators, using her goals and time horizon.

Time Out

Please note that these are before tax rates of return. They are only approximations. Your actual rate of return will vary depending on the performance of the investments you actually invest in.

1. Her $15,000 lump sum investment, with an additional $500 a month invested systematically, will grow to $31,905 at a rate of return of 10 percent. This will pay for her graduate education and provide the down payment on her home purchase.
2. Her $5,000 money market account will have grown to $17,600. She will be saving about $1,000 a month in taxes (due to mortgage write-off), which she will then begin to add to her monthly investment program. She then intends to invest $1,500 a month in mutual funds ($2,000 of the total will go into her IRA and be tax-deferred).
3. We determined that in order to retire at age sixty and have an annual income at retire of $36,000, she will need to save approximately $750,000. By investing $1,500 a month for the following twenty years she will have accumulated $833,000, which will provide her with the income she desires for retirement.

If after inputting your numbers on the calculator the results indicate that you have a shortfall, the calculator will automatically tell you what you'll need to do to alter the plan so that it works out for you. The calculator will provide you with the following feedback:

- How much more you need to invest to accomplish your goal.
- The rate of return you'll need to earn on your money to meet your goal.
- How much more time is needed to accomplish your goal if none of the other factors are changed.

Example: If you can only save $5,000 a year toward your retirement but you need a minimum of $3,000 a month to retire comfortably, the calculator will indicate what you need to do to get on target. It will tell you that you'll need to either save an additional amount per year, invest differently to achieve a specific rate of return, or, if nothing changes, wait an additional number of years to retire.

As you are working on your financial plan keep in mind that you will find it easier to accomplish your goals if you can save versus spend. Your summary of income and expenses should be carefully reviewed if your calculations indicate you are unable to meet your goals. What can you do to reduce your spending now so that you can have what you want later? If we really think about it, most of us waste money on things that are not that important to us. It is important to put you're spending into perspective. If your goals and objectives are really important to you, you might need to sacrifice a latte here and there and drive a less expensive car. Live a more manageable life today so that your future isn't spent before you get there. Here are some tips for saving that can really add a lot to your investment dollars.

Just a Minute

An alternative to doing these calculations online is to hire a financial planner or investment professional to do this planning for you for a fee. A list of resources for this is included in the reference section of this book.

Always think before you spend.
Bring your lunch to work.
Consciously conserve energy.
Decide what really matters.
Eat in.
Forfeit the little things, they add up.
Go camping; it costs little and it's lots of fun.
Have a garage sale every year.
Invite friends over for a potluck.
Just do it at home. Do you really need a gym?
Keep a log of your daily spending. See where it goes.
Living on less means living better longer.
Make it; don't buy it.
Never buy retail when you can get it wholesale.
Be open to the possibility that you don't need so much "stuff."
Play outdoors; it's good for you and doesn't cost a dime.
Question your motives for wanting something you don't need.
Read more.
Spend less, buy in bulk.
Take the bus or train if it saves you money.
Use your skills or hobbies to make more money.
Visualize what you want everyday so you don't forget.
Waste nothing.
Your money will grow if you invest it, otherwise it just goes.
Zzzzzzz . . . always be wide awake and alert while trading online.

At this point you should have created the template of your financial plan that fully incorporates your goals and objectives. It should consist of taking the money you have to work with currently (taken from your net worth statement) with money you have left over each month for investing (taken from your summary of income and expenses) and entered into the appropriate financial calculator. The results will have provided you with an expected outcome or map to where you're headed if you proceed as planned.

Now it's time to begin looking at specific investments and decide where to invest your money. Before you begin choosing your investments, here's a piece of investment advice that you can put up on your refrigerator to use as your investment mantra:

To risk everything is risk losing everything. To take some risk usually results in some rewards and some losses. To risk nothing is to stand still and go nowhere, which is perhaps the greatest investment risk of all. To risk this is to merely "go broke slowly."

CHAPTER FOUR

Investment Choices and Asset Allocation

I'm living so far beyond my income that we may almost be said to be living apart.

—E. E. CUMMINGS

Now that you have created a financial plan and know what your basic investment strategy will be, it is time to make specific investment choices and create an asset allocation plan. It is absolutely essential that you complete this next step before you begin investing. In order for an asset allocation to be done correctly, it must be tailored to fit *your* investor profile. There are many financial Web sites that provide asset allocation planners to assist you with this process. The most common asset allocation models are designed to fit the needs of the prevailing investor profiles, which are:

- ultra-conservative investor
- conservative investor
- moderate investor
- moderately aggressive investor
- aggressive investor

Based on the work you did in the previous chapter, you should have a good handle on what your investor profile is. The next step is to decide which investments best suit your profile and then allocate your money accordingly. Later in this chapter we will go online and look at some asset allocation planners. Before we do that, let's make certain that you understand the major investment choices available to you. The types of investment options this chapter will cover that can easily be traded online are:

- stocks
- bonds
- mutual funds
- initial public offerings (IPOs)

It is important that you understand what each of these investments is and how it works before you make your final investment decisions.

What Is a Stock?

Common stock is a security, issued in shares, that represents ownership in a corporation. These shares are sold on the market exchanges to the public. Common stockholders have voting rights and may receive dividends after all other obligations are paid.

Preferred stock is stock issued by a corporation to the public in the form of shares. Preferred shares pay a dividend that must be paid prior to dividends paid to common stock holders. Preferred stock may be exchanged for common stock. It may also be callable, often at a price that is at a premium (higher) than the par value (or current price). Owning a callable security gives the issuer the right to redeem the investment. Should this occur, your principal and any unpaid dividends will be paid in full.

Shares of both common and preferred stock represent ownership in a corporation. The basic difference between these stocks is that common stockholders have voting rights and preferred

Helpful Hint

As an investor, the main reason you would buy a preferred issue over common stock is for income. If you are mainly interested in growth, common stock is probably your best choice.

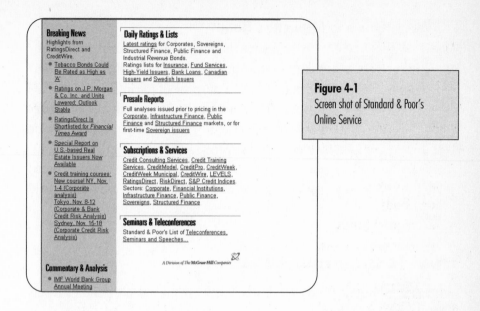

Figure 4-1
Screen shot of Standard & Poor's Online Service

stockholders give up their right to vote, choosing instead to receive a fixed dividend.

What Is a Bond?

GOVERNMENT BONDS

Government bonds are debt securities issued by the government in order to raise money through borrowing from investors. The investors who purchase these bonds are paid periodic interest payments and repaid their principal investment at the end of a stated period of time. These bonds are issued in a variety of denominations and with various maturities. The interest income received is generally subject to federal taxes but can be exempt from state and local taxes depending on the issue.

CORPORATE BONDS

Corporate bonds are debt securities issued by corporations in order to raise capital by borrowing from investors. These bonds also pay an agreed interest rate for a stated period of time, or if they are callable, until they are called. Corporate bonds are issued in a variety of face amounts and maturities. The income received is fully taxable.

Time Out	

Bonds are rated by credit agencies. It is important to inquire about a bond's rating before you buy it. Issues with no or low credit ratings may be somewhat illiquid or very volatile.

MUNICIPAL BONDS

Municipal bonds are debt securities issued by state and local governments or municipalities (thus the name) for the purpose of raising money by borrowing. They are generally issued in denominations of $5,000 or greater. They offer a wide variety of maturities. An investor in muni bonds receives periodic interest income for a stated period. At the end of this period they are repaid their principal investment.

What Is a Mutual Fund?

In general, a mutual fund is a professionally managed portfolio of assets that is open ended, that is, it has no maturity and can be redeemed at any time. Mutual funds are diversified and each has a stated objective or purpose that must be strictly adhered to, which is stated in the prospectus. A prospectus is the terms and conditions, so to speak, of the mutual fund and its company operations.

TYPES OF MUTUAL FUNDS

- Bond Funds
- Tax-Free Bonds
- Growth Funds
- Growth and Income Funds
- Balanced Funds
- Sector Funds
- Specialty Funds
- Index Mutual Funds
- International Funds

TYPES OF MUTUAL FUNDS

Bond Funds

Bond funds are mutual funds that invest in government or corporate bonds with the objective of providing consistent income to their shareholders in a diversified portfolio.

Tax-free bond funds have the same objective as regular bond funds, but they invest in municipal bonds for the purpose of providing a tax-free income flow to their shareholders. Income on municipal bond funds are free from federal tax but may be taxed at the state and local level. Some issues are completely tax-free.

Growth Funds

Growth funds invest primarily in common stocks for the purpose of appreciation versus income. These portfolios attempt to manage assets for the highest rate of return while minimizing the risk by being diversified and disciplined in their strategy.

Growth and Income Funds

A growth and income fund can be diversified in a variety of ways, from primarily dividend producing stocks to a combination of stocks and bonds, depending on the manager. The overall intention is to provide some income to investors without sacrificing the potential for growth.

Balanced Funds

Balanced funds are invested in both stocks and bonds for the purpose of total diversification.

Sector Funds

Sector funds are invested in a particular industry or type of security. They can be invested in stock sectors, precious metals, oil and gas, real estate, or any industry sector. These funds can be more volatile or speculative depending on whether a particular sector is in or out of favor with the economy.

Index Funds

Index mutual funds are mutual funds that invest in the stocks of a particular index such as the S&P 500, the Dow 30, the S&P 100, etc. Management does not attempt to beat the market by picking their own stocks, but rather invests in the "leaders" of a particular index.

International Funds

International funds invest in companies outside the United States. Some international funds invest in many different countries; others will specialize in a particular country or geographic region.

Initial Public Offerings

An initial public offering (referred to as an IPO) is a stock that is being issued to the public by a corporation that is "going public." IPOs are considered highly speculative and can be very volatile with wide fluctuations in price.

Asset Allocation

Now that you have a good working idea of the types of investments that are available to you online, you can begin to select investment types that fit into your plan. This is called an asset allocation. Asset allocation is the process of selecting and allocating your money in a manner that would best match your financial objectives with your investor profile.

You will be able to find many different asset allocation models on the Internet, or, if you're working with a professional advisor, he or she can

Figure 4-2
Asset Allocation Models

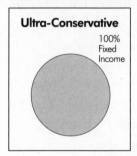

Ultra-Conservative

100%
Fixed
Income

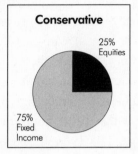

Conservative

25%
Equities

75%
Fixed
Income

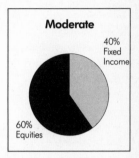

Moderate

40%
Fixed
Income

60%
Equities

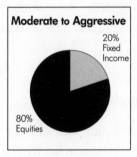

Moderate to Aggressive

20%
Fixed
Income

80%
Equities

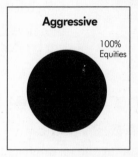

Aggressive

100%
Equities

assist you with this as well. For purposes of this lesson, however, see the following sample asset allocation models.

In selecting investments, there are four important considerations:

1. Do you need income from your investments now?
2. Do you have the time to pick and manage your own individual stocks?
3. Are you more comfortable with a managed investment such as mutual funds?
4. How much money, if any, are you interested in being more speculative with?

Helpful Hint

The purpose of these allocation models is simply to give you ideas about how to diversify your money into different types of investments. If you aren't the kind of person who likes charts and graphs, you don't need to have a pie chart done like this. These models are just visual representations of an asset allocation.

Choosing Income Investments

The rule of thumb regarding income investments, especially bonds, is this: the higher the yield, the greater the risk. High-yield bonds (also known as junk bonds) can provide a great return on your money, but you should have a fairly high risk tolerance. If you don't mind principal fluctuation, high-yield bonds can produce a higher income flow than other bond funds with higher credit ratings. However, it is essential that you do your research here because ratings and performance history are critical facts. Not all high-yield bonds are created equaly.

Choosing Individual Stocks

Trading individual stocks can be a lot of fun and very rewarding if you don't mind doing the research and the potential volatility. The markets are moving faster than ever before, so be prepared. If you stick with solid growth stocks, you'll be okay in the long run as long as you stick to your plan. When it comes to long-term results, nothing outperforms growth stocks. That is simply a fact.

In one of the best historical perspectives ever conducted, Jeremy Siegel, professor of finance at the Wharton School of Business, goes back as far as 1802 to prove that no other single investment has ever outperformed growth stocks, regardless of the economy or political environment throughout time. In his book, *Stocks for the Long Run*, Jeremy Siegel makes the most compelling case for stocks that this author has ever read. Not only does his academic study indicate that stock returns far exceed any other investment over this long span of time, but he also clearly demonstrates that growth stocks are probably the safest investment as well.

According to this historical study, the longer you plan to hold you investments (i.e. need them to grow), the safer growth stocks are. For the purpose of portfolio allocation, for example, the risk tolerance charts in this book indicate that even ultraconservative investors could safely allocate 41 percent of their portfolio to stocks if their intention was to hold the investment for at least ten years. A conservative investor could invest up to 61 percent in stocks; the moderate investor could invest as much as 86 percent; and the aggressive investor could allocate 100 percent.

Smart Investor Tip

Stocks for the Long Run should be on your list of "must read" investment books.

According to author Jeremy Siegel, this is how stocks compared to other investments:

If you had invested $1 in growth stocks in 1802, it would have grown to 9.1 million dollars.

This is how that same $1 in other investments grew over the same period of time:

Bonds grew to $12,656
Treasury Bills grew to $3,859
Gold grew to $13.57

While these figures are nominal rates of return and do not show the impact of taxes and inflation, the numbers are still quite staggering. Although this information may help you to consider investing in individual stocks, the bottom line when it comes right down to it should still be: What are your goals and what are you comfortable investing in? Keep that in mind in choosing your investments.

Helpful Hint

If you don't have the time or are not interested in managing individual stocks, you should either hire someone to do it for you (you can still have online access if you choose an advisor whose broker/dealer offers online trading). In Chapter 7 you will learn more about choosing an advisor, should you decide you need one.

Choosing Mutual Funds

If you're not comfortable with individual stocks, for whatever reason, mutual funds are a great alternative investment choice. Mutual funds offer such tremendous flexibility and variety of choice that it's hard to go wrong if you choose

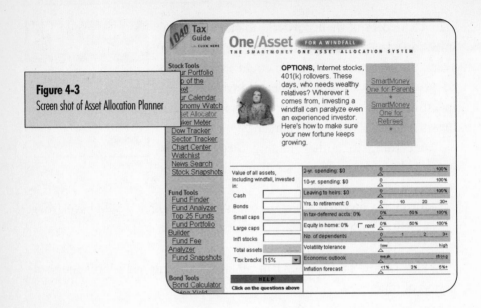

Figure 4-3
Screen shot of Asset Allocation Planner

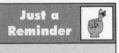

Just a Reminder

You should always choose funds that match your investor profile that is in line with your goals and time horizon.

highly rated investments with good long-term track records.

In creating your asset allocation, you will need to decide what percentage of money you are going to allocate into which types of investments. To assist you with this process, you might want to go online now and use the asset allocation planner shown below.

We'll use our previous example, Ms. Smith, a moderate to aggressive investor, to walk you through this. Ms. Smith allocated her money in the following manner:

50% in individual growth stocks
10% in small cap growth stocks
20% in growth mutual funds
20% in international mutual funds

This portfolio is completely suitable for Ms. Smith's investor profile. Even though over half of her portfolio is in individual stocks, she chose well-known, large cap growth stocks, which should help her accomplish her goals provided she sticks to her plan.

Now it's time for you to choose what percentage of your money will go to which investments. You won't be making specific investment decisions until later.

To wrap up this chapter, let's recap what you should have accomplished by now. You should know:

- Your goals and objectives.
- How much money you need to invest to accomplish each of your goals.
- How much you'll need to earn on your money to reach your goals.
- How much time it's going to take you to reach your goals.
- How much money you intend to allocate to which types of investments in order to reach your goals.

If you've completed all of these processes, congratulations! You not only have a basic financial plan, you now have completed your asset allocation, which will serve as the road map to your financial future.

Just a Reminder

The purpose of this exercise is to help you complete your game plan. That way, when you get to the point of actually selecting investments you'll know where to begin your research and how much money will be going to which investments. Knowing this before you get started will save you a lot of time. You don't want to spend hours researching mutual funds if you're fairly certain you want to have the majority of your money allocated to individual stocks. Conversely, you don't want to spend a lot of time on stock research if you know you need monthly income, in which case you should be researching bonds or bond mutual funds that pay out monthly.

Time's Up

Let's test your readiness. Take this quiz.

1. If you needed $1,000,000 in order to retire comfortably in twenty years, how much money would you need to save per year and at what rate of return? (Use your online calculator.)
2. If you need your investments to provide you with a monthly income immediately, what types of investments should you be looking at to provide that for you?
3. If you are a moderate investor with $25,000 to invest over the next five years, approximately how much will your investment grow to in that period of time, assuming a 10 percent return?
4. What investment vehicle has outperformed all other investments over time?
5. How much money should you invest speculatively if you have a conservative investor profile and would not handle it well if you lost money?

ANSWER KEY:

You can find the answers to questions 1 and 3 by using your on-line calculator skills.

#2.   Although some individual bonds pay monthly, they can be hard to find. Bond mutual funds will generally provide the best source of monthly income. Most other income producing investments, such as preferred stock, pay semi-annually or quarterly income distributions.

#4.   High quality growth stocks have outperformed all other investments over time.

#5.   Zero. If you have a conservative investor profile you should not be investing speculatively at all.

CHAPTER FIVE

Rules of the Road

An expert is someone who knows some of the worst mistakes that can be made in his subject and who manages to avoid them.
—WERNER HEISENBERG, 1969

This chapter will familiarize you with the rules and regulations you need to know regarding trading securities. By the end of this chapter you will have a working knowledge of the laws that are pertinent to you as an investor. It is important to remember that these laws are in place to protect you and your investments. This chapter will make researching easier and safer. Before long, making trips to the SEC's Web site to check out investments will be second nature.

Investment Industry Regulation

The investment business is one of the most highly regulated industries in the United States. Such heavy regulation is necessary in order to create an orderly marketplace and to protect the investing public. Otherwise, quite frankly, the stock market would become total chaos and the viability of investments sold would be questionably higher than it is. Strong regulation is even more essential than ever given the explosive growth of online trading.

As a result of rules and regulations set forth by the SEC, investors are able to trust, for example, that Microsoft is a real company and a legitimate investment not simply because a) Bill Gates, the owner of Microsoft, is a very public person b) we have to use his software in order for our computers to function properly, and c) he has more money than God, so Microsoft must be worth something of value. The main reason you can rest assured that Microsoft and other publicly traded companies are real entities is due to SEC registration requirements. All publicly traded stock is required to be registered with the Securities and Exchange Commission (a.k.a. the SEC), which is the main governing body of the securities and investment industry.

Main Laws Governing the Industry

The Securities Act of 1933 was the first law enacted by Congress pertaining to the regulation of the sale of securities. Also referred to as the Truth in Securities Act, this law requires the full disclosure of all material facts about corporations who sell stock to the public. As a result of this law, a corporation must disclose its history, financial background, and background of its officers and directors in a document referred to as the registration statement. This must be completed prior to the initial sale of its stock to the public. Corporations are also required to provide a prospectus, or written offer to sell, to the purchasers of the security. The registration process is quite complicated and requires that an established procedure be followed before a corporation may issue its stock to the public for sale. These are the steps a corporation must follow:

- Filing of the preliminary registration statement with the SEC.
- The SEC examines the registration statement and if all is in good order declares an effective date for the offering of the stock.
- A "due diligence" meeting is held, during which time indications of interest are taken from potential buyers.
- If required, a preliminary prospectus (called a "red herring") is distributed.
- The syndicate meets to negotiate the price of the issue, creates a final prospectus, and prepares the offering. The syndicate is a group of investment firms organized to prepare and sell the security to the public. They also assume the financial risk of a new stock issue.
- Once the preliminary prospectus and registration statement have been filed with the SEC, a waiting period known as the twenty day "cooling off period" is initiated (although the SEC can lengthen or shorten this time frame, if necessary).
- Toward the end of the waiting period, an effective date is set after which the stock issue may be sold to the public. Prior to the actual sale of the stock, a final registration statement and final prospectus must be filed with the SEC, clearing up any deficiencies pointed out by the SEC in the preliminary documents.

As you can see, a corporation has to jump through a lot of hoops to issue publicly traded stock. A company must be perceived as a credible investment in order to receive the support and financial commitment it needs from the investment community. This support is critical to ensure the offering is successfully sold. It is essential that investors understand this process so that they can have confidence in the market and in their investment choices. Understanding how the investment marketplace works will help you become a better investor.

Trading Practice Laws

The Securities Exchange Act of 1934 was the next law created that affects everyone who trades securities. This law governs the rules of disclosure and self-policing with respect to the buying and selling of securities traded on the public exchanges. The primary purpose of this act is to prohibit acts of misrepresentation, manipulation, and other types of abusive trading practices in the securities market. This law also regulates the securities exchanges, broker/dealers, and investors.

Inside Information

As an online investor, it is important to be aware of certain laws and how they apply to you. One of the main laws that people are often misinformed about is inside information. Trading a security on information that is not available to the general public is illegal. Inside information is clearly defined as "any material fact about a company that has not yet been made public information." Anyone, not just an officer or director of a company (referred to as an "insider"), can be held responsible for the buying and/or selling of a security on the basis of inside information. If anyone ever offers you a so-called tip or passes a rumor to you regarding a company, do not participate in the information. The spreading of tips and rumors is strictly prohibited.

Manipulation and Fraud

The 1934 Act strictly prohibits any fraudulent or deceptive sales or trading practices. Although this law is intended to govern the sales practice of the securities industry, it can apply to individuals as well. Such prohibited practices include:

- concealment of information
- exaggerations or false claims
- intentional misrepresentation
- promises of gain
- material omissions of fact or information

It is unlawful for any individual to manipulate a security through buying or selling in a manner that creates a false appearance of active trading. This type of activity could influence other investors to buy or sell the same security purely on the basis of manipulation. One example of a manipulative trading practice is called "painting the tape." This type of trading involves the simultaneous buying and selling of the same stock (with no real change in ownership), which causes multiple trades to appear on the tape. Such increased activity in the stock could attract buyers or sellers and influence the price of the stock.

"Penny Stock" Rules

In 1990, the SEC made it illegal for broker/dealers and their representatives to cold call or solicit potential investors regarding the sales of "pink sheet" stocks selling for under $5 per share unless the following information was strictly adhered to:

- Proper and adequate financial information was obtained from the prospective investor.
- Written information was sent to the prospective investor with an explanation regarding the appropriateness of the investment.
- An order to buy the investment cannot be placed until the prospective investor sends back a signed suitability statement and verification of financial information.

Delivery of Securities

If you sell a security, such as a stock or bond, and have possession of the certificates of ownership, you are required to deliver your certificates in good form, properly endorsed, and on a timely basis. Failure to do so can cause restrictions on your ability to trade.

Time Out

If someone solicits you to buy a penny stock, make sure the disclosure statement includes the current bid and asking price, as well as the commissions earned. Also, bear in mind that penny stocks are considered very speculative, so tread this area with caution. In general, it is best to consider the solicitations of these types of investments as potentially suspect. Many of the recent scams in today's market are related to small company stocks traded (or falsely said to be traded) on the "pink sheets." That is not to say however, that these types of investments are all bad. This is just a word of caution: do your research and check out these types of issues thoroughly before you invest.

Settlement of Trades

When you place an order to buy a security, you are required to "settle" the transaction on a timely basis. In a cash account, "regular-way" trades settle on the third business day after the trade was placed. Under Reg-T, you must pay for your trades within five business days. An extension for up to seven days may be made, but no longer.

If you fail to pay on a timely basis, your broker/dealer will sell out your account the day after the settlement was due. "Buy-ins" may occur ten days after the original settlement date. If you violate any of these rules your account can be restricted for ninety days without the cash in your account.

Helpful Hint

In the event that you do buy a stock and then sell it prior to paying for it, you should be aware that the brokerage firm will not release the funds from the sale before they have received payment. Once the funds are received, they will first offset the payment made against the debit for the purchase or sale.

Free-riding or Withholding

If you habitually buy and sell securities before paying for them you run the risk of violating securities law for something called free-riding. This kind of buying and then quickly selling, without putting any money up, is effectively using the broker/dealer's money for personal gain and is illegal. It is prohibited for anyone to have more than three transactions of this type in a twelve-month period before the account becomes restricted.

Margin Accounts

One of the most complicated and troublesome areas of the securities industry is margin trading. Most brokerage account forms include a section regarding their margin agreement but it is often overlooked or not properly understood by the investor. You could easily sign a new account form and agree to open a margin account without knowing it. Although most brokerage firms have attempted to make this part of their agreement more clear, it has been a problem in the industry. This is a real life example.

Several years ago I was referred to a woman by a professional organizer who had become suspicious of her client's broker due to an increase in activity on her account statements. I was asked to meet with the client to review her statements. During this review, I asked the woman where her income was coming from, and she replied, "Oh, I live on the money in my money market account. I usually keep about $100,000 in that account."

I asked her if she had a money market account elsewhere since the statement I was looking at did not have any funds in her money market account. She did not. It was at that point that I had the unpleasant task of informing this poor woman that not only did she not have any cash left, but she had a margin debit balance of over $100,000.

This woman became a client of mine and upon further investigation, we discovered she had signed a margin agreement when she opened her account with her previous brokerage firm. It basically gave her broker the ability to borrow against her portfolio to buy other investments. Whenever this broker called to advise her of an investment opportunity, she gave him the go ahead, not realizing he was borrowing to buy. To add insult to injury, most of the investments lost money, while the client was being charged 11 percent interest to buy investments she really could not afford.

In the end, the client hired a securities lawyer in Los Angeles to file suit on her behalf. Between her margin account debit and poor investments, this unfortunate woman lost over $600,000. Approximately four years later her lawsuit was settled in arbitration and she recovered less than $100,000. If she had not signed the margin account agreement (even though she was unaware of what she had signed), most of her losses could have been avoided in the first place.

Margin Rules

These are the rules on margin trading that you should become familiar with if you intend to trade on margin:

The federal government will not allow a brokerage firm to loan or margin more than 50 percent of the value of the securities held in the account. Firms generally establish their own in-house rules regarding the amount they will loan on margin, but it can never exceed 50 percent. The line of credit or loan extended to a customer is called the SMA (Special Memorandum Account). This is the amount that is available to purchase securities on margin. This amount will vary from day to day depending on the actual value (or equity) of the securities pledged as collateral in the account. Margin limits may also vary from one brokerage firm to another.

Regulation T

Reg-T is the law that governs the amount and type of credit a broker/dealer may loan to its clients. In addition to the 50 percent rule, there are additional requirements that must be adhered to.

These rules include:

- The account must maintain a minimum of $2,000 in equity at all times.
- If the client purchases or withdraws securities in excess of his or her buying power, the client will receive a margin call.
- A margin call, known as a "T-call," requires that money be deposited into the account to cover the call within five business days. An extension allowing up to seven days may be allowed.

The formula for margin calls is this:

Reg T requirement – SMA balance = Margin Call

Example: If you were to buy 100 shares of IBM at $200 a share in a margin account, the Reg-T margin requirement would be 50 percent of

$20,000 ($200 x 100) or $10,000. If the market dropped and IBM fell, you would receive a margin call if your debit balance, or amount owed, exceeded your buying power, or SMA limits, required by your broker/dealer. You would then be required to deposit funds to cover this margin call. Industry standards require that a client's equity must be at least 25 percent of the long market value of the securities held in the account and may never fall below $2,000. If you fall below these minimum requirements you would receive what is called a maintenance call or "house call," which means you would have to deposit funds to bring the equity in your account back up to the 25 percent rule.

Increased Maintenance Requirements

In light of the recent volatility of the markets overall, some broker/dealers are increasing their maintenance requirements for margin accounts that have more volatile stocks.

This is a precautionary effort being taken in order to reduce the potential risk and exposure associated with these stocks. This requirement helps to ensure that customers will have sufficient equity in their accounts to cover too large of a price fluctuation. The maintenance requirement increases have ranged between 40 to 100 percent for long positions and even greater on short positions on option trades.

Helpful Margin Formula

In general, this is the formula you can use to help determine the maintenance requirement in your account if you are trading on margin (unless otherwise stated or notified by your broker/dealer):

Long Market Value (equity in your account)
- *minus your Debit Balance (amount you owe)*
= *Equals Equity of your account*
- *minus 25% maintenance requirement*
= *equals Maintenance excess*
(amount of credit available to be borrowed) or
Maintenance deficiency (amount you are required to deposit)

Marginable Securities

Not all investments can be purchased on margin. Under Reg-T, only securities that have a loan value are considered marginable. The following is a list of marginable securities:

Leveraging your portfolio assets can be a great investment strategy if you know what the rules are and fully understand the cost and risk associated with this kind of trading. In fact, if you are a very savvy investor, you might actually make a lot of money trading this way. Again, knowledge is the key to success in this game.

- Any security or bond that trades on a national securities exchange.
- Any open-ended investment trust that is registered *and* has been held in an account for a minimum of 30 days.
- Any stock that trades on the NASDAQ.

Restricted Accounts

If you have a margin account that has less equity than your initial margin requirement, or your debit balance (amount you owe) exceeds your equity, your account will become restricted. In addition to receiving a margin call, any sales made in your account will be applied to reduce your debit balance first. You will only be able to use up to 50 percent of the value of your SMA account.

Example: You decide to sell IBM because you've made a nice profit and have decided to use the proceeds to buy a new car. Wrong. If your debit balance exceeds the equity in your account, 50 percent of the proceeds from the sale of your IBM stock will immediately go to reduce your debit balance. You can only use half of the IBM proceeds to buy the new car.

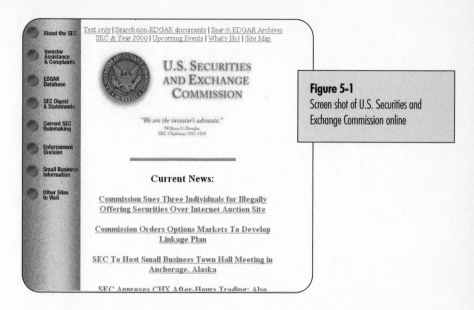

Figure 5-1
Screen shot of U.S. Securities and Exchange Commission online

An account may also become restricted for other reasons:

1. Failure to pay for the purchase of a security.
2. Failure to deliver a security (stock or bond certificate, for example) following its sale.
3. A habit of buying and selling a security before payment was actually made (referred to as "free-riding").
4. An account automatically becomes restricted when the owner of the account dies (except in joint accounts with rights of survivorship).
5. In the event of death, all open account orders are cancelled, the assets are frozen, and the account remains restricted until written legal instructions are received from the administrator or executor of the deceased client's estate.

While there are many other laws in the investment industry, the rules that have been outlined in this chapter are the ones that you as an investor should be most familiar with. If you ever have any questions about these rules and regulations, it is important that you speak to someone first before you act. If you do not have access to a financial or legal advisor, contact the Securities and Exchange Commission's public information line at 800-SEC-0330. You'll find them very willing to assist you with any questions or concerns you might have.

PART TWO

CHOOSING

AN

ONLINE

TRADING

PARTNER

CHAPTER SIX

Types of Online Trading Companies

Science finds, industry applies, man conforms.
—ANONYMOUS, SUBTITLE OF GUIDEBOOK TO
1933 CHICAGO WORLD'S FAIR

In this chapter you will become familiar with the various types of online trading companies available on the Internet. Although these companies continue to grow in number and their features and benefits change almost daily, this chapter will provide you with important parameters to consider, regardless of these frequent evolutions. By the end of this chapter you will be ready to choose your online trading partner. You will be equipped with the following information to assist you:

- types of online brokers
- trading costs
- services offered and fees
- deposits required
- security provided
- investment options available
- research capabilities
- service support

The rapid growth of online investing has exceeded all predictions. It is difficult to believe the first initial public offering (IPO) appeared on the Internet just a few years ago in 1995. Andrew Klein, the CEO of Spring Street Brewing Company, a New York microbrewery, had the audacity to sell shares of his company directly from a Web site. The SEC was taken aback by this innovative initial public offering and questioned Klein about his online venture. Fearing legal action, the brewery voluntarily withdrew the offering and suspended trading. A short time later, Klein was notified that the SEC planned to take no action against his IPO.

> **FYI**
>
> The SEC didn't realize it at the time, nor did anyone else, but by taking no action against Klein's IPO they were essentially waving a green flag of approval (some say it was a white flag) for online securities trading.

It was then off to the races for brokers that previously had only dabbled with online trading via primitive computer/modem or touch-tone phone connections. E*Trade, *www.etrade.com*, which provided a rudimentary online trading presence since 1992, opened a formal Web site in 1996 and saw 40 percent of its customers trade directly at the Web site. Charles Schwab, who has offered a limited trading platform since 1984, immediately stepped up its online presence. Charles Schwab opened its Web site *www.schwab.com* in May of 1996.

Rapid Rise in Online Traders

Customers flocked to online broker Web sites in record numbers. By the end of 1998 there were over eighty online security brokers for customers to choose from. However, since the Internet and online trading were so new to both customers and the industry itself, there was no criterion by which to distinguish one broker from another. Consequently, with little else to differentiate the first Web sites except cost, a price war broke out. Low cost was considered the primary way to attract new customers and retain old ones. Today, one online firm, Brown and Co., offers market trades for a flat rate of five dollars, exemplifying the lasting effect of the price war.

All of a sudden there was a shortage of webmasters to quickly put together attractive and informative Web sites for brokerage houses. Time was of the essence. "Get a Web site or be left in the dust!" was the fear. Today, thankfully, there are more criteria by which to judge an online trader than just low cost.

You get what you pay for. This adage applies to online trading partners as well. If you feel confident enough about a stock to make a simple market trade with little or no assistance, more wealth to you, but keep in mind that assistance before and after the transaction comes in many subtle yet important ways. This level of assistance can be used as a yardstick to determine whether an online broker is a deep-discount, discount, or a full-service brokerage.

Deep-Discount, Discount, and Full-Service Brokers

Keep in mind that there is a gray line between the definitions of these three types of brokerages and generalizations are hard to avoid, especially since online trading is evolving on a daily basis. Furthermore, many brokerage firms actually have three levels of service and cost, thereby placing them in all three categories. Firms that cost-wise qualify as a deep-discount broker might very well offer a particular service that is usually only provided by full-service brokers, for instance, real-time quotes.

DEEP-DISCOUNT BROKERS

Deep-discount brokers are commonly considered brokers that offer market trades for less than $14.95 for between 100–500 shares.

DISCOUNT BROKERS

Discount brokers execute market trades for between $15 and $19.95 for 100–500 shares.

FULL-SERVICE BROKERS

Full-service brokers charge $20 and upwards for trading between 100–500 market shares.

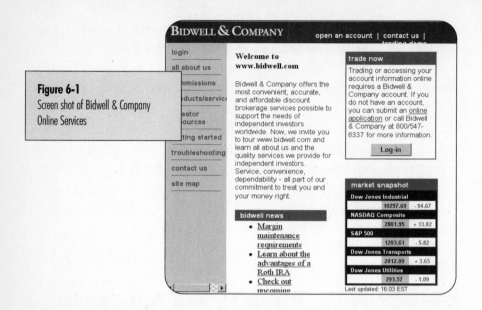

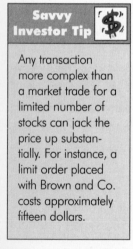

Figure 6-1
Screen shot of Bidwell & Company
Online Services

Considerations in Choosing an Online Trading Partner

TRADING COSTS

It is imperative that the online investor fully understands the true cost of using an online broker. Many brokerages entice the cost-conscious shopper to their Web site with sharply discounted commissions for simple market trades. Just as a grocery store attracts you to their store with loss leaders (a can of tuna for 49 cents), so too do online traders.

> **Savvy Investor Tip**
>
> Any transaction more complex than a market trade for a limited number of stocks can jack the price up substantially. For instance, a limit order placed with Brown and Co. costs approximately fifteen dollars.

ADDITIONAL COSTS

Another method that helps deep-discount and discount brokers cover their costs (for trades over and above a simple market trade) is to assign a cost for bookkeeping and documentation fees that would otherwise be free at a full-service broker. The extra charges can quickly turn what seemed like a bargain transaction into an expensive proposition. Some of the cost items provided below by Bidwell and Company might be essential for you as an online trader.

Miscellaneous Online Fees:

Confirmation, statement, and 1099 replacement	One free, $5 each additional
Early Trade Payment	$25 or interest
Foreign security transfer	varies
IRA annual fee	$25
Issuance of third party checks	$5
Late payment	$5 plus interest
Late receipt of securities sold	$5
Legal transfer fee	$25
Limited partnership transfer	varies
Mailgram margin notices	$25
Overnight delivery	$15
Registered delivery of certificates	$10
Reorganizations	$25
Restricted stock transfer	$50
Returned check for NSF	$25 plus interest
Stop payment of check	$20
Wire transfer domestic/foreign	$15/25

MINIMUM DEPOSITS

Remember that online brokers require minimum deposits of anywhere from $2,000 to $15,000. You should keep your reserve funds in a money market accounts or other income-producing sources until such time as you direct them to specific investments.

ONLINE SECURITY

Online security over the Internet has improved greatly in the last few years. Up-to-date

Helpful Hint

When shopping for an online securities broker, keep in mind that a small commission charge for a simple market trade can quickly escalate and chisel away at your profit.

Internet navigation software, such as Netscape Navigator and Windows Explorer, can now be downloaded for free at their respective Web sites. When downloading the software it is highly recommended that you choose the most secure version available. Netscape, for example, periodically updates and enhances their browser software. Most brokerages state that the buyer should use only the latest software from Microsoft or Netscape.

Online security is provided automatically when using the latest security-enhanced software. All e-mail messages and orders are automatically encrypted with complex codes similar to those used by the armed services. A hacker would have to work days on end with a mainframe computer to crack an encryption code. Likewise, most brokerages use software that encrypts messages sent to you and between their trading partners.

FYI

Guard Dog is also capable of warning you of potential viruses that are trying to infect your computer. Many other virus protection software packages are also available. It is highly recommended that you choose one and upgrade it frequently.

Supplemental security software is also available through various companies. One software program that gets good reviews is Guard Dog. This program warns you any time a Web site attempts to send you a cookie. A cookie is a trail a Web site leaves behind on your hard drive that allows them to track your Internet activity. Generally, this cookie is left for marketing purposes, but many users find this an invasion of privacy. Programs like Guard Dog, by Symmantec Corp, can warn you when a Web site you visited tries to leave a cookie on your hard drive. It also gives you the option of refusing the cookie. Netscape also has a feature that if activated will warn you of cookies. You will be given the option of accepting, rejecting, or returning the cookie.

USE SECURE BROWSERS

Don't take for granted that a financial transaction between you and your trading partner is secure and confidential. Confirm the online security capabilities of any and all brokers before you conduct business with them. Never release personal information such as your social security number, account information, or street address before affirming that security is in place.

INSURANCE

Make sure that your trading partner is properly insured. It only takes one clever hacker to gain access to your entire portfolio. Investment industry insurance is most commonly provided by SIPC (Securities Investment Protection Corporation.) Most accounts are insured for a maximum of $100,000 in cash and $500,000 in securities.

DELAYED TIME QUOTES VS. REAL-TIME QUOTES

The ability of a broker to furnish you with real-time quotes can be crucial if you are a day trader or have a strong hunch about an IPO. Seconds count if a stock is hot! If a stock is moving up or down rapidly you must know and be able to act immediately. The market can be extremely volatile, as we all learned in the last year. Time is of the essence!

Real-time quotes are quotes that generally appear on your broker's Web site within fifteen seconds of their live posting at a particular exchange or market. Verify in writing what your trading partner means by real-time quotes. Furthermore, the online broker you deal with should guarantee that your transaction will be posted immediately. Many brokers deal with traders that must verify each transaction before posting and this can delay a transaction for hours. Other brokers guarantee that if your transaction isn't filled within ten seconds there is no charge for the trade.

> **Helpful Hint**
>
> It is also important that your account is updated with real-time quotes. It is impossible to manage financial holdings wisely if your account status isn't punctually updated.

Many firms offer unlimited, free real-time quotes as part of your account for a monthly fee. Other firms allow you only a limited number of free real-time quotes. Still other brokers do not offer access to real-time quotes at all. If you access real-time quotes on any plan other than a free, unlimited basis, you must monitor your account for extra charges. It may be cheaper to switch to a plan or brokerage that offers free, unlimited real-time quotes.

TRANSACTIONS HANDLED

Many deep-discount and discount brokers don't offer a full selection of products. Deep-discount and discount brokers can be compared to shopping at a convenience store. Brand selection and quality is sufficient at best. But if you're not into shopping and know exactly what you want, a bag of chips, a can of dog food, etc., convenience stores fill a necessary

Just a Reminder

Avoid the compulsion to buy or sell stocks simply because you can do so at bargain commission rates. You may soon find yourself addicted to the same adrenaline rush that fuels gamblers at the Las Vegas casinos. Resist the temptation to abandon your strategy simply because you can change your mind for $5 and a simple mouse click.

market niche. The same is true with brokers who don't offer a full array of financial products. Don't go there unless your list of needs is short and basic.

MARKET TRADES

All online traders offer market trades at varying prices. This is one online transaction where a shopper can truly save on commission charges because the online broker's overhead is lower for this transaction.

FUTURES

Not all brokers handle futures and not all traders should buy futures. Trading commodities is a risky transaction best left to experts or traders directly involved with a particular commodity. For example, Starbucks Coffee purchases futures in raw coffee to guarantee a profit margin at the retail level. Without a doubt, the coffee buyers at Starbuck's spend untold hours studying climactic conditions, crop reports, world economies, etc. before they invest in coffee futures. Unless you are willing to spend countless hours researching the futures market and take significant financial risk, stay out of this market.

BONDS

Even though bonds are offered by many online brokers, the wise investor should spend some time getting to understand the various types of bonds available and their inherent risks before investing. Investors attracted to bonds are usually looking for a secure investment with a reasonable rate of return. To rush into the bond market online without proper consideration and perhaps, if warranted, the advice of a professional defies the very logic that attracted you to bonds in the first place. Remember, you can't actually trade bonds online by yourself. You will need to contact your online broker for assisstance in buying or selling bonds. It will cost you extra to do this.

MUTUAL FUNDS

Each online broker has a list of mutual funds that they offer, along with a fee schedule. If you intend to invest a substantial part of your money in mutual funds, choose an online broker that has extensive selling agreements with a wide range of mutual fund families. Remember that track record is everything when choosing a mutual fund or fund family to invest in, so do your research.

Point of Reference

For more assistance on mutual funds, go to Chapter 13. It will assist you further in your search for the perfect mutual fund.

RESEARCH CAPABILITIES

Research! Research! Research! If you expect to make money buying and selling securities online you must research your decisions. Hunches are stimulating but in the long run you will lose more than you will win. With the advent of sophisticated broker Web sites and search engines, there is no excuse for a buyer not to do research. Access to research is usually an extra charge at deep-discount brokers. Many discount brokers include limited research in their somewhat higher commission schedule.

Just a Reminder

Careful scrutiny must be paid to the fine print concerning the cost of research fees. A plan that charges by the hour can quickly add zeros to your commission fee.

CRASH PROTECTION AND MORE

In the event that a computer crashes and you are unable to access your online account, there should be an alternative system in place. eBay, the online auction company, had four crashes in June and July of 1999. Millions of dollars were lost in commissions and nerves were frayed. Within weeks of the crashes new online auction sites popped up on the Internet, capitalizing on the customer dissatisfaction with eBay. Of course, eBay's stock took a dive after each incident. Time will tell if the damage is permanent. If eBay had alternatives and backup systems in place the damage could have been minimized.

When selecting an online broker check into pre-existing backup systems. A backup system might be as archaic as a local walk-in office or a

Helpful Hint

A customer can easily test the level of customer support at a brokerage house by actually sending an inquiring e-mail or phone message before opening an account. Keep shopping until the response time and service are sufficient.

touch-tone phone. Crashes are inevitable and frequent enough to warrant a broker maintaining two concurrent Web sites, or possibly just a primitive backup Web site that can handle emergency orders.

SUPPORT, OFF AND ONLINE

Poor service is the most common complaint against online brokers. Specifically, customers charge that their brokers fail to respond promptly or effectively to e-mail, phone calls, or letters. A low-cost broker can translate to low profit margins, which often results in poor customer service due to a lack of personnel.

Partial List of Deep-Discount Brokers

(All prices are per trade unless otherwise noted.)

AF Trader	$14.95 and up
Ameritrade	$13 (limit) or $8 (market)
Brown	$10 (limit) or $5 (market) and up
Datek	$9.99 and up
Empire	$14.95 (limit) or $11.95 (market) and up
Firstrade (First Flushing)	$9.95 and up
ForbesNet	$9.95 and up
InvesTrade	$11.95 (limit) or ($7.95)
Muriel Siebert	$14.95 and up
MyDiscountBroker (Sovereign)	$12 and up
Prestige Status	$13.90 and up
Scottsdale (Scottrade)	$12 (limit) or $7 (market)
Suretrade	$9.95 (limit) or $7.95 (market) and up
Trading Direct	$9.95
TruTrade	$12.95
UMC–United Management Corp.	$14.95 and up
U.S. Rica Financial	$12.50
Vision Trade	$10.95 and up
Waterhouse (Kennedy-Cabot)	$12
A.B. Watley	$9.95 and up
Web Street	$14.95 (sometimes less)
Jack White (merger with Waterhouse in process)	$12 and up

Partial List of Mid-Cost Discounters

(All prices are per trade unless otherwise noted.)

1st Discount Brokerage	$17.75 and up
Active Investor	$15 and up
BCL Online	$18 (limit) or $13 (market) and up
Bidwell Express	$16.25 and up
Bull & Bear	$19.95 and up
Citicorp Investment	$19.95
Discover	$19.95 (limit) or $14.95 (market) and up
Dreyfus	$15 and up
E*Trade	$19.95 (limit) or $14.95 (market)
Freedom	$15
Freeman Welwood	$19.95 (limit) or $14.95 (market)
GFN (Gay Financial Network) Investments	$19.95 and up
Investex	$17.95 (limit) or $13.95 (market) and up
InvestIN.com (RT Day Trading)	$17.95 (limit) or $14.95 (market) or $19.95 (day trade, limit) or $18.95 (day trade, market)
InternetTrading.com	$17.50 and up
J.B. Oxford	$18 (limit) or $13 (market) and up
Lindner Funds/FarSight	$17.95 (limit) or $14.95 (market) and up
Main Street Market	$19.95 (limit) or $14.95 (market) and up
Mr. Stock	$19.95 (limit) or $14.95 (market) and up
MyTrack	$15.95 (limit) or $12.95 (market)
N.D.B.	$19.75 (limit) or $14.75 (market) and up
Newport	$19
Preferred Trade	$15 and up
Quick & Reilly	$19.95 (limit) or $14.95 (market) and up
Sanford Securities (Australian stocks only)	$16.80 and up
Stocks4Less	$17.50 (limit) or $10.50 (market)

Trade4Less	$19.95 and up
TradeOptions	$15 and up
Tradestar	$19 (limit) or
	$14 (market)
U.S. Discount Brokerage (USDB)	$19.95
Wall Street Discount	$19.95 and up
Wang Investments	$8 (limit) or
	$5 (market)
Wit Capital	$19.95 (limit) or
	$14.95 (market) and up
Wyse	$15.45 per GTC trade or
	$12.45 per limit day trade
Ziegler Thrift	$19.73 and up

Partial List of High-Cost Discounters

(All prices are per trade unless otherwise noted.)

Accutrade	$29.95 and up
A-1 Financial	$24.95 and up
American Express	$24.95 and up
Andrew Peck	$24 and up
Atlantic Financial	$55 per trade
Beckman	$20 and up
Bush Burns	$25 (limit) or
	$20 (market) and up
Castle	$20.95 (listed) or
	$19.95 (NASDAQ) and up
Clark Financial	$39 and up
CompuTEL	$21.50 (limit) or
	$16.50 (market) and up
DLJ Direct	$20 and up
E*Trade Canada	$38.88 and up
FarSight	$20 and up
Fidelity	$30 (limit) or
	$25 (market) or
	$19.95 (active traders, limit) or
	$14.95 (active traders, market) and up
Frontier	$33 and up
Green Line	$39 and up
ML Direct–Merrill Lynch Online	$29.95 and up
Net Investor	$20.95 and up
Nowtrade (Wisechoice)	$23 (limit) or
	$15.95 (market) and up
Olde	$20 and up

Peremel	$20 (limit) and $18 (market) and up
Regal	$26 and up
Schwab One	$29.95 and up
Sunlogic	$48 (limit GTC) or
	$18.99 (market) and up
Swiftrade	$32.50 and up
Trade-Well	$25.50 and up
Vanguard Brokerage	$20 and up
Wall Street Access	$26.50 and up
Wall Street Electronica	$21.95 (listed) or
	$19.95 (OTC) and up
Wall Street Equities	$24 (limit) or
	$15 (market) and up
Wilshire	$15 and up

You have now had the opportunity to assess the different types of online trading companies available. Before making your final decision, it is important to take into consideration which type of online broker best meets your needs as an investor. If you are tempted to make your selection only on the basis of cost, you may find yourself unhappy with the outcome. To conduct further research, refer to some of the recent reviews from well-respected newspapers and magazines such as the *Wall Street Journal*, *Forbes*, or *Worth* magazine.

CHAPTER SEVEN

With or Without Professional Advice

No man's knowledge here can go beyond his experience.
—JOHN LOCKE, *AN ESSAY CONCERNING HUMAN UNDERSTANDING*, 1690

This chapter is dedicated to helping those of you who are uncertain about investing online. In this chapter we will take a close look at your options. There are a variety of professional advisors who can assist you with critical financial decisions. Many of these advisors offer online trading as well, which for some investors is the best of both worlds. This chapter will help you to decide what works best for you.

Historic Changes in Online Trading

Less than one year ago, most major full-service brokerage companies were scoffing at the possibility of participating in the online trading business. As far as they were concerned, online trading was contrary to their way of doing business and it was not perceived as a threat to the status quo. Online trading was frowned upon as little more than child's play in what has always been a fiercely competitive "old boy's" network.

In early July of 1999, a story was leaked to the *Wall Street Journal* that Merrill Lynch, the largest brokerage firm in the nation, had plans to launch an online trading site by the end of the year. The *Wall Street Journal* initially advised Merrill of their intention to print this story, giving them twenty-four hours to prepare, but the story hit the front page news before Merrill had the opportunity to inform their over 15,000 brokers of the news.

Smart Fact
According to research conducted by the TowerGroup, an Internet technology research and consulting firm, a record number of 32.7 million accounts are projected to be trading online by the year 2001. That represents of increase of over 25 million people since 1997.

As a broker with Merrill Lynch on the day this story went public, it became clear that the full-service brokerage business as we had known it was forever changed. In the days that followed another fact became transparent. If Merrill Lynch was about to jump on the online bandwagon, then the existing online trading business was considered a threat. The word around the company was that this was war. Merrill was not going to just stand by and watch their online competitors beat them at their own game.

Meanwhile, most other major brokerage firms were either caught with their pants down or were prepared to announce that they, too, would be joining the ranks of Merrill Lynch. To date, Salomon Smith Barney, Prudential Securities, and PaineWebber have announced plans to launch online trading sites. Some companies such as Morgan Stanley Dean Witter are already up and running.

Future Impact of Changes

Given the billions of dollars at stake and the powerful infrastructure of the investment community, it remains to be seen how the smaller online trading firms will survive amidst the might of the giants. A company like Merrill Lynch, for example, has the single largest distribution system in the world at their fingertips, that is, as long as they can keep their brokers happy and well compensated. This too remains to be seen. Most stockbrokers at firms like Merrill are still wandering the halls in shock trying to figure out how they're going to be compensated under the new system.

By all accounts, the difference that established brokers are counting on to help them beat their new online competition is the availability of professional advice and service. To their credit, this is something full-service brokers have the experience and infrastructure in place to provide that the discount companies simply cannot afford to offer.

How to Choose an Advisor

As an individual investor it can be difficult to sift through the volume of information and choices available to choose from in today's investment marketplace. You can choose anything from one-stop shopping, where you can get all your financial needs and products met under the umbrella of a single firm, to the lowest possible trading cost of $5.95 per stock order (as of this date, anyway) with little or virtually no service at all.

To determine whether to invest with or without professional advice, ask yourself these important questions?

1. What kind of financial advice do you think you need?
2. How much time do you have to dedicate to doing your own investing?
3. How much is it worth to you?
4. What can you afford to spend?
5. What are you willing to spend?

Guidelines to Consider

Here are some guidelines for you to consider. The more money you have, the more complicated your financial picture is, generally speaking. Unless you have an enormous amount of free time *and* really enjoy delving into financial data, it would probably behoove you to at the least pay for a financial advisor to help you to develop a financial plan and/or estate planning, depending on your net worth. In truth, most individuals with a high net worth cannot afford *not* to hire a professional unless they personally are trained and educated in the field. Why? Because not getting the right advice can be a costly mistake. A good professional will save you much more money as a result of good advice than he or she will ever cost you. It really is that simple.

Here's a good example. Mrs. Jones, age fifty-five, becomes widowed and is the beneficiary of an estate valued at five million dollars. Mr. Jones took very good care of business, invested well, and left his wife financially well off. He did not however, do any estate planning, so some critical estate planning issues were passed on to his wife.

Mrs. Jones left money matters to her husband. She has no financial background or investment experience. She has two adult children and several grandchildren. If she does not receive good advice soon, much of the money her children and grandchildren could have inherited will be forfeited to the I. R. S. in federal estate taxes. Now if Mrs. Jones just decided to jump online, she would run the risk of either:

A. Becoming a victim of a online investment scam
B. Investing in unsuitable investments
C. Investing too speculatively
D. Not being properly diversified

That being said, if Mrs. Jones pursues the advice she needs, does some estate planning, and begins to become more educated about investing, she could easily open an online account and invest her own money if she were so inclined. However, if she simply skipped the advice part and moved straight into managing her own money, she would cost herself and her family literally millions in unnecessary estate taxes. To do this in order to save money on commissions and fees is foolhardy.

If we change the picture a bit and make this woman a thirty-five-year-old computer programmer who just inherited $50,000 from an aunt, the story would be different. A thirty-five-year-old has a lot of time ahead of her to learn and can afford to make some mistakes. She also has earning power, which Mrs. Jones does not. (Mrs. Jones must live off of her investments as her sole source of income.) The computer programmer, due to her occupation, is already computer savvy so online investing is not a stretch for her. And although the amount of money at risk is not insubstantial, she could easily figure out how to carefully manage it on her own through reading this book and conducting her own research. Her financial picture at this stage in the game is not terribly complicated and millions are not at risk. Wisely invested, her investment nest egg could grow into an amount that would someday require professional advice.

Cost Versus Value

It is necessary to have perspective on the cost versus the value of what you're getting in life. You should only be willing to pay for advice that you can see a direct benefit to. If you're not reaping some rewards from your financial advisor's efforts and advice (given a year or two to perform), then you should fire them, hire a new one, or do it yourself. You need to have an agreement about what to expect, realistically, from an advisor and then make them accountable for meeting or exceeding these expectations.

Do You Need Advice?

Knowing when you need advice is the key. For example, I know that I am entirely capable of doing my own tax return. I am not, however, a tax expert. Because of my profession I may know more about taxes than the average person, but my knowledge is limited and I do not have time to become an expert. Consequently, I have an accountant do my taxes for me. Without fail, every year my accountant finds something that I didn't catch. In the long run, I am certain he has saved me a lot of time, money, and tax problems. I have a doctor and a lawyer for the same reason. It's called "an ounce of prevention."

Consider Your Time

People are busier than ever before. The media bombards us with volumes of information on ways to be even busier doing it ourselves. There is a "do it yourself" guide for virtually everything. The problem is, when does anybody have the time? When it comes to professional financial advice, you should really consider time as a factor of utmost consideration. If you have very little spare time now, how much time can you allocate to learning about and becoming your own investment advisor? If you don't have the time, then you really owe it to yourself to get the advice you need.

Savvy Investor Tip

Smart Investors knows when they're in over their head and should seek the advice of a professional. If a pipe breaks in your house, you would call a plumber. Don't you think your financial future deserves at least as much consideration as a busted pipe? Some things are better off attended to by those who are trained to do the job.

Helpful Hint

Get referrals to advisors that have helped others you know and interview each of them until you find the right fit. If financial planners also provide investment products, they should disclose that they also receive commissions.

Types of Advisors

There are many types of financial advisors that you can use to assist you, depending on your needs. These are some of the professional advisory services available to you, what they offer, and how they generally charge:

CERTIFIED FINANCIAL PLANNERS (CFP)

Some financial planners charge an hourly fee to do an in-depth financial plan; others charge a flat fee. Today, financial planning software has made it easy for the big brokerage firms to provide financial plans as well, at a lesser cost. For example, Merrill Lynch charges $250 for a basic financial plan, which is about one-fourth the cost of a plan provided by an independent planner. The plan alone, however, is not very valuable if it doesn't come with good advice and direction on how to implement it. You should give some thought about who is best suited to provide you with objective feedback on how to attain your financial goals.

FINANCIAL CONSULTANTS AND INVESTMENT ADVISORS

I throw this group into a single category for one reason: they are basically the same. Financial professionals can call themselves just about whatever they want to as long as they are licensed to do whatever it is that claim to be. This is somewhat confusing to the public, however. As a rule of thumb, most people in this category make their income from providing both advisory services and selling investment products. Usually, the advice is free and you can call these advisors whenever you need to without being charged. The investments these advisors put you into are usually their sole source of compensation. The expertise of this group of professionals varies highly from one person to the next.

Good questions to ask a potential advisor in this category are:

How long have you been in business?
What licenses or credentials do you have?
What is your investment philosophy?

Are you restricted as to the types of investment companies or products you can offer?

How are you compensated?

Do you have references I can call?

You should be able to ask any potential advisor all of these questions. If someone resists or is evasive in responding, you should think twice before using his or her services. A good financial advisor will not hesitate to answer all of your questions. They should want you to be informed and be interested in having a long-term relationship with you. If they are just out to sell you something, you should move on.

Most of my clients have been with me for many years, some for as long as I have been in business. These clients rarely concern themselves with my fees because they're satisfied with the results my advice has given them. Recently, a client who has worked with me for over ten years called me to complain about the ticket charge on a stock transaction I had placed for her. It was a purchase of 100 shares of Broadcom and it cost her $115. A month later, when she called to complain about the cost, she had already made 50 percent on her money (an unusually high return for such a short period). I had charged her full markup (1.5 percent of the purchase price) due to the amount of research time I spent reviewing this stock. As a result, her $115 cost made her a profit of over $12,000 dollars. I asked her if she was thought this was a fair exchange? The answer, of course, was yes.

> **Exception to the Rule**
>
> If the stock market has a major correction during the first year or two after you've just begun investing with an advisor, you should not be overly concerned if your portfolio has not met your expectations (unless your losses are far greater than average). Chances are your portfolio would be down no matter whom you invested with. No advisor can predict or prevent these market corrections. You need to be prepared to ride them out.

FEE-BASED MANAGEMENT CONSULTANTS

A growing breed of investment advisor has begun to carve a market niche into helping investors choose professional asset managers (some of whom were previously only available to very high net worth individuals). In return for helping you choose a manager that meets your profile, needs, and objectives, the advisor charges an annual management fee. This fee is divided between the advisor and the asset management firm. This type of advisory service may very well be the wave of the future. Here are reasons to consider a fee-based advisor:

1. It's cost effective and there are many options to choose from that are not readily known to the general public. The cost to hire a fee-based advisor runs between 1 to 2 percent of the amount invested per year, depending on the advisor and the manager.
2. These types of asset managers do not have a sales force, per se. They are dependent on the investment advisor to bring them new business. If they lose the confidence of the advisor, they lose their future business.
3. Because the fees are paid annually, if you or your advisor are not happy with the manager, you can fire them and hire a new one without incurring a sales charge (in most cases).
4. These managers must perform in order to maintain their client base. Performance based advice is always the best advice. It keeps everyone on thir toes and accountable.

ONLINE FULL-SERVICE BROKERS

There are several full-service firms with online sites (refer to the previous chapter for details on these sites). However, almost none of them offer online trading yet. This is anticipated to change slowly over the next year. Some companies have opted to wait until after the year 2000 and any complications associated with Y2K have been resolved. As it stands, Merrill Lynch and Smith Barney will be offering unlimited online trading for accounts over $100,000 in assets for a fee (between $1,200–$1,500 annually). The fee includes unlimited access to a financial consultant as well as many other features and benefits that were previously cost items. Clearly, this segment of the market is looking to attract customers with spending power. All of the full-service brokerages firms are still offering their advice without a fee but with the standard higher commission structure.

To summarize, the most valuable benefits of having a financial advisor are personalized service from someone who knows you, financial advice, investment guidance, strategic planning, and advice and assurance during volatile market cycles. These are some of the reasons you might want to consider using a professional. The important thing to remember is this: You can do both. If you need advice, get it. If you still want to trade online, do it.

Doing one does not rule out the option of utilizing the other. This is one of those situations in life where you can have your cake and eat it too. The choice is yours and whatever you choose is not permanently written in stone. If you try it one way and it doesn't work, you can always try another approach. One thing is certain: the investment world is changing daily and there is literally something for everybody. It's okay to experiment a bit until you discover which way is right for you.

Exception to the Rule

Most full-service brokerage firms also offer fee-based services as well, such as financial plans and fee-based asset management consulting. You can choose which of these programs works best for you.

CHAPTER EIGHT

Opening an Online Account

All sufficiently advanced technology is indistinguishable from magic.
—ARTHUR C. CLARKE, 1972
THE LOST WORLDS OF 2001

You have finally arrived at the point in this book when you can safely and knowledgeably open an online account. By the time you've reached this chapter you should have chosen an online trading company and be ready to complete the new account form. This can be done, in most cases, online or off. In either case, this chapter will walk you through the entire online application process.

All online brokers are required by law to have you fill out an account application form. The application form satisfies the SEC requirement that all brokers know their clients' financial status for proper management. Avoid the temptation to quickly fill in the blanks. The application is for your protection. Your ability to effectively and swiftly make online trades is determined by how you answer these questions. How you fill in the blanks can also have a profound effect on your income and taxes. To fully comprehend the repercussions of how an account application is opened with an online trader it is necessary to study a typical application line by line. This one is used by Ameritrade.

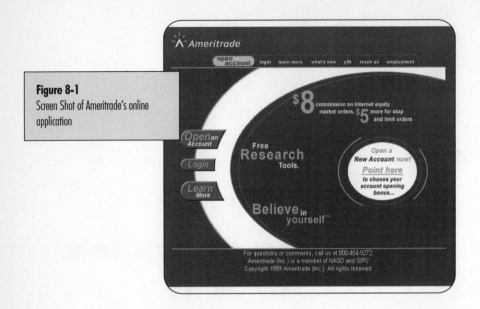

Figure 8-1
Screen Shot of Ameritrade's online application

Types of Accounts

Types of accounts include individual, joint, corporate, IRA, custodial, retirement, and trust. Keep in mind you are not opening a video rental account here. The box you "X" here can be as important as the investments you make.

INDIVIDUAL

An individual account means only you have the right to access this account. It means your spouse, siblings, and attorney cannot manage the account, even in emergencies, without a power of attorney. If you uncertain due to personal circumstances whether an individual account is the right choice for you, seek the advice of a financial advisor or CPA.

JOINT ACCOUNT

One or more individuals, all of whom have a right to individually or collectively trade securities on this account, may open joint accounts. In the event of the death of one of the account holders, titles to securities in this type of account become the sole property of survivors named on said account. Only individuals who have the utmost trust in one another should open joint accounts.

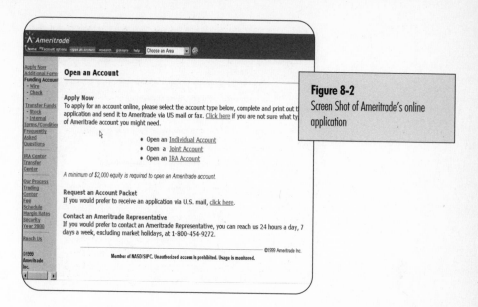

Figure 8-2
Screen Shot of Ameritrade's online application

Custodial Account

Minors are not allowed to manage their own money or trade securities until they reach the age of eighteen or twenty-one, depending on state statutes. Custodial accounts for minors fall under the Unified Gift to Minors Act (UGMA) or Unified Trust for Minors Act (UTMA). When the minor child comes of legal age, the account automatically becomes his or her sole property. Until the minor is of age an adult custodian must manage the account in a responsible manner. Recently there have been some high profile minor versus custodian lawsuits that revoked the custodial power from the parents because of mismanagement of funds. As a custodian of a minor's account, you are acting in a fiduciary capacity. Legally, this means you have the responsibility to invest prudently on behalf of the minor.

Helpful Hint

It is advisable that you consult a financial advisor or lawyer regarding title issues of custodial accounts. All custodial accounts must be titled according to UTMA or UGMA. There are both legal and tax implications to be considered. Example of a custodial account title: John D. Smith, Custodian for John Smith Jr., under UGMA.

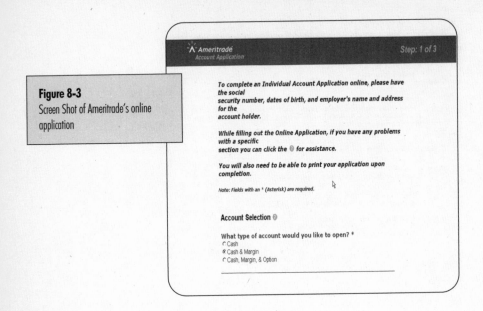

Figure 8-3
Screen Shot of Ameritrade's online application

To complete an Individual Account Application online, please have the social
security number, dates of birth, and employer's name and address for the
account holder.

While filling out the Online Application, if you have any problems with a specific
section you can click the ⓘ for assistance.

You will also need to be able to print your application upon completion.

Note: Fields with an * (Asterisk) are required.

Account Selection ⓘ

What type of account would you like to open? *
 ⃝ Cash
 ⦿ Cash & Margin
 ⃝ Cash, Margin, & Option

TRUST ACCOUNT

Trust accounts are excellent tax havens that provide for loved ones in the future. Don't scrimp here and hastily set up an online trust account without personally speaking to a financial advisor or attorney.

In most cases, a trust protects the privacy of an estate and its beneficiaries and helps to avoid the costly and often lengthy process of probate. There are many types of trusts, each serving a distinct purpose. For assistance regarding what type of trust is most suitable for your estate, consult an estate-planning attorney who specializes in this area of planning.

CORPORATE

Corporate accounts are reserved for businesses that are incorporated in the United States. Proof of incorporation will be required to open this type of account. Of course, investments purchased by a corporation are owned by the stockholders of the corporation.

IRA

IRA accounts are relatively easy to open online, but keep in mind that if you open a self-directed IRA account you will have to manage it yourself as you would any other investment. If you are uncomfortable managing

Account Funding ⊘

How do you plan to fund your account? *
☐ Wire
☐ Check
☐ Transfer
☐ Stock Certificates
☐ Transfer from existing Ameritrade Account

Account Holder Information ⊘

First Name *

Middle Name

Last Name *

Address Information ⊘

Physical Address *
(P.O.Boxes Not Accepted)

Mailing Address - (If different)
(P.O.Boxes Accepted)

Figure 8-4
Screen Shot of Ameritrade's online application

your own retirement plan, professionally managed IRA accounts are easily obtained online at most full-service brokerages.

RETIREMENT

Retirement accounts generally require the services of a full-service broker. Since there are many different types of retirement accounts, it is advisable that you consult a financial advisor or CPA to ensure that you choose the most advantageous plan.

Financial Fact

A tax break is a terrible thing to waste. Retirement accounts can help reduce your tax liability and allow you to invest more toward retirement. Take advantage of favorable tax laws now. You never know how long they'll last.

Types of Accounts—Cash, Margin, or Margin with Options Trading

A cash account means the online broker has your cash on hand to make the trades you desire. Cash accounts restrict a buyer's ability to acquire securities with a purchase price above what is on deposit with the broker.

A drawback to a cash account is that by the time more monies are deposited with the online broker, that hot stock you wanted to buy may

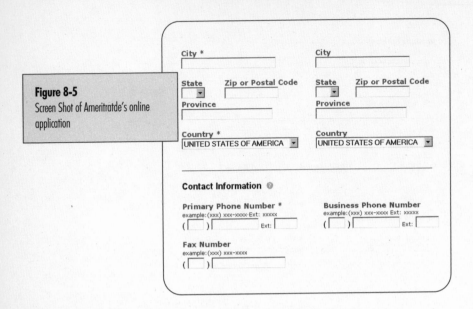

Figure 8-5
Screen Shot of Ameritratde's online application

no longer be hot. If you are planning to do much trading, have the money available in your online account. It can be earning interest in a money market account until you need it for placing a trade.

MARGIN ACCOUNTS

Margin accounts and margin accounts with options allow a buyer of securities to purchase more securities than are actually in an account with the online broker. The SEC is particularly concerned that online investors do not fully understand the implications of opening a margin account. In a memo dated July 22, 1999, the SEC warns investors:

> *Be wary of buying stock on margin. Make sure you understand how a margin account works, and what will happen in the worst case scenario before you agree to buy on margin. Unlike other loans, like for a car or a home, that allow you to pay back a fixed amount every month, when you buy stocks on margin you can be faced with paying back the entire margin loan all at once if the price of the stock drops suddenly and dramatically. The firm has the authority to immediately sell any security in your account, without notice to you, to cover any shortfall resulting from a decline in the face value of your securities. You may owe a substantial amount of money even after your securities are sold.*

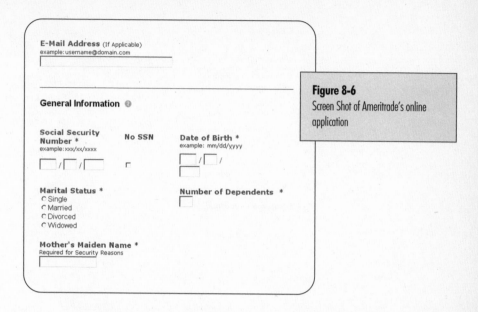

Figure 8-6
Screen Shot of Ameritrade's online application

Furthermore, the SEC is concerned that online brokers are not informing their online clients about the risks involved with margin accounts. During high-volume trading sessions brokers have little time to personally advise a client that a particular trade is risky. The SEC found that during volatile market sessions, especially involving Internet-related stocks, many online brokers were ill-equipped to make punctual and accurate transactions for their clients, let alone inform them of risks involved.

Initial Deposit

To attract new clients some brokers offer new accounts with no initial deposit. Of course, it is futile to open an account with no deposit because the account cannot be utilized until monies are on account. The hope is that once you open an account you will eventually deposit money or securities with the broker. E*Trade requires a $1,000 minimum deposit for cash accounts and a $2,000 deposit for margin accounts and margin accounts with options trading. Online brokers such as E*trade generally only accept personal checks, money orders, or cashier's checks for cash accounts. Remember, deposits must clear the bank before monies can be used for transactions. Security certificates and transfer accounts are also accepted, but because they require more time to transfer, your first online shopping spree may be hampered.

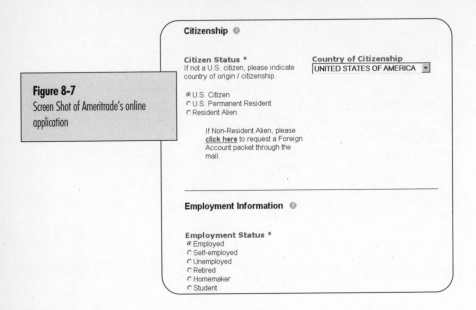

Figure 8-7
Screen Shot of Ameritrade's online application

A transfer from one brokerage firm to another can take anywhere from seven to fourteen days, that is, if the transfer forms are received in good order and the online firm's back office is efficient. It is not uncommon for transfers to be delayed for unreasonable periods of time. Meanwhile, for as long as the transfer is in progress, you do not have access to the funds. You cannot buy or sell any securities in the account until the assets are received and the transfer is complete.

Your Name (First, Middle, and Last)

Use your complete and true name here. Your account security depends on accuracy and completeness. Also, if you are transferring your account, the name on both accounts must read exactly the same.

Street Address

Most brokers require a real street address, not a P.O. box. Be accurate here in the event that hard copy documents require immediate attention and signing. You can add a P.O. box as a mailing address if necessary.

If you selected "Employed" or "Self-Employed", you must enter in
an Occupation.

Occupation
[   ]

The following information is required only if you selected
"Employed".

Employer Name
[   ]

Employer Street Address
[   ]
[   ]

City
[   ]

State   **Zip or Postal**
                   Code
[▼]   [   ]
Province
[   ]

Country
[UNITED STATES OF AMERICA   ▼]

Figure 8-9
Screen Shot of Ameritrade's online
application

E-mail Address

E-mail is the fastest and least expensive method to
send and receive correspondence from your
broker. E-mail can be sent and received within seconds. Check your e-mail at least once a day to
ensure that your online brokerage account receives
the attention it deserves.

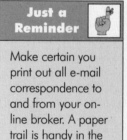

**Just a
Reminder**

Make certain you
print out all e-mail
correspondence to
and from your on-
line broker. A paper
trail is handy in the
event of a dispute.

Phone Numbers

Correctly list your home and business phone numbers here or risk not
being notified by phone when your account needs immediate attention.
List any other pertinent numbers where you can be reached (vacation
homes, cell phones, etc.) if you tend to be difficult to track down.

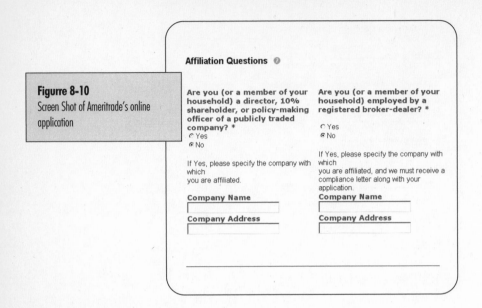

Figurre 8-10
Screen Shot of Ameritrade's online application

Affiliation Questions @

Are you (or a member of your household) a director, 10% shareholder, or policy-making officer of a publicly traded company? *
  ○ Yes
  ● No

If Yes, please specify the company with which
you are affiliated.

Company Name

Company Address

Are you (or a member of your household) employed by a registered broker-dealer? *
  ○ Yes
  ● No

If Yes, please specify the company with which
you are affiliated, and we must receive a compliance letter along with your application.

Company Name

Company Address

Social Security Number

The social security number listed here should match the name (names) on the account. Today, many businesses, public and private, identify a person and accounts by social security number rather than name. Correct social security numbers are essential for correct IRS reporting. If your name and social security number do not match, your account may be flagged and become subject to backup withholding or other account restrictions.

TAX I.D. Number

Corporations, partnerships and trusts usually use a tax identification number in lieu of a social security number. You must use one or the other to open an online account.

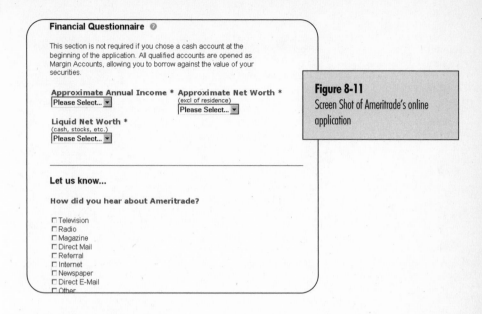

Financial Questionnaire @

This section is not required if you chose a cash account at the beginning of the application. All qualified accounts are opened as Margin Accounts, allowing you to borrow against the value of your securities.

Approximate Annual Income *   Approximate Net Worth *
[Please Select... ▼]   (excl of residence)
                                         [Please Select... ▼]
Liquid Net Worth *
(cash, stocks, etc.)
[Please Select... ▼]

Let us know...

How did you hear about Ameritrade?

☐ Television
☐ Radio
☐ Magazine
☐ Direct Mail
☐ Referral
☐ Internet
☐ Newspaper
☐ Direct E-Mail
☐ Other

Figure 8-11
Screen Shot of Ameritrade's online application

Date of Birth

This line establishes that you are considered an adult in your state and can legally engage in trading with a licensed broker.

Country of Legal Residence (U.S. Citizen, Resident-Alien, Non-Resident Alien)

If you are not a U.S. citizen you may be required to provide additional documentation to prove your country of residence. Alien status does preclude one from opening an online account with a United States stock brokerage.

Your Employment (Employer and Occupation)

This question helps the broker to assess your income level and financial savvy.

Figure 8-12
Screen shot of inside trading from Yahoo!

The table shown in the figure:

Insider Trades - The Walt Disney Co (NYSE:DIS)   Updated: 11-Oct-99

Date	Name	Action	Shares	Type	Price	Value
g-99	DISNEY ROY E	Gave as Gift	10,835	Common	-	-
g-99	DISNEY ROY E	Holdings	770,208 (i)	Common	-	-
-99	BOWERS REVETA FRANKLIN	Exercised (M)	550	Common	17.89	-
18-Jun-99	DISNEY ROY E	Gave as Gift	32,982	Common	-	-
7-May-99	AHMANSON CAROLINE L	Sold (S)	20,000 (i)	Common	30.32	$606,400
30-Apr-99	BOWERS REVETA FRANKLIN	Acquired (J)	146	Common	29.92	-
31-Mar-99	BOWERS REVETA FRANKLIN	Acquired (J)	117	Common	37.41	-
16-Mar-99	DISNEY ROY E	Gave as Gift	976	Common	-	-
5-Mar-99	COOKE JOHN F	Sold (S)	210,000	Common	35.69 - 35.87	$7,516,860
5-Mar-99	COOKE JOHN F	Exercised (M)	210,000	Common	17.58	-
5-Mar-99	COOKE JOHN F	Planned Sale (144)	210,000	Common	-	$7,300,000
9-Feb-99	LITVACK SANFORD M	Sold (S)	63,000	Common	34.25	$2,157,750
9-Feb-99	LITVACK SANFORD M	Exercised (M)	63,000	Common	9.56	-
9-Feb-99	LITVACK SANFORD M	Holdings	2,703 (i)	Common	-	-
8-Feb-99	LITVACK SANFORD M	Sold (S)	211,000	Common	34.25	$7,226,750

Business Address

This question must be answered to open an account. If you are self-employed, an employee, or not employed, you must indicate something on the application or it will be rejected.

Employed by Broker/Dealer

Licensed brokers and their employees are allowed to open accounts at other brokerage houses, but their employment must be revealed on the application. If you fall into this category, you should know that your employer will be notified and sent statements of your account activity. The account may be personal or business related. This question is asked as a precaution against insider trading and fraudulent activity.

Director

Are you a director, 10 percent shareholder, or policy maker for a publicly traded company? If you answer "yes" to this question it doesn't preclude you from trading with an online broker. However, it does send up a red flag that you are in a position to easily commit the crime of insider trading. Also, all transactions involving the firm that you represent must be reported to the SEC for evaluation. If a director, major shareholder, or policy maker for a publicly traded company makes a trade of company stock, the information is public knowledge and is frequently published by financial news services.

Investment Objectives

The main categories of investment objectives are capital preservation, income, growth, and aggressive growth. This information helps satisfy the SEC requirement that a broker know the financial objectives of their clients. How well a broker can know a client from this question is a subject of great debate. However, it does give the broker a rough idea what investments you should be investing in and which investments are out of character with your financial goals. Since it is difficult for online brokers to truly know their customers, more and more online brokers are requiring you to sign a binding arbitration agreement. This can limit judgments against the brokerage but saves both parties huge legal fees.

> **FYI**
>
> Studies show that most clients who took their cases before arbitration boards only received approximately 28 percent of the amount they felt they deserved.

Investment Experience

The possible responses to this question are none, limited, good, or excellent. This information gives the broker an idea of investments that might be suitable and attractive to you. It also tells the broker that complex and/or risky investments need to be explained in detail. Keep in mind that online brokers are dealing with hundreds of thousands of clients. Unless you are with a full-service broker, do not expect personalized service, regardless of how you answer this question. They simply don't have the time or personnel to hold the hand of every novice online investor and walk them through the pros and cons of a particular municipal bond. This is why many deep-discount brokers are requiring you to be an experienced trader with years of investment experience. This way the broker's potential for lawsuits is greatly reduced by ensuring that their online clients are responsible for their own financial transactions.

What Type of Investment Accounts Do You Have?

This question gives the online broker a picture of your investment experience and suitability for future investments. It also gives the broker an idea of the type of investments you prefer. If you answer "yes" to owning any of these investments it is very likely that you will be contacted by a broker (if you're with a full-service broker) to discuss your willingness to transfer these investments to his or her brokerage house.

By now you have learned everything you need to know about opening an online account. Hopefully, before you actually open the account, you will have given this decision the utmost consideration. It is easy to be enticed into the online trading world by attractive Web sites and the apparent ease of opening an account. In addition, the bull market of recent years and its unprecedented profits is attracting thousands of financial novices to low-cost, online brokerages. However, the decision to open an online account should be made judiciously. Do not deposit your hard earned money just anywhere or without reading the fine print.

PART THREE

TOOLS

OF

THE

TRADE

CHAPTER NINE

The Best Online Research and Publication Sites

Man is still the most extraordinary computer of all.
—JOHN F. KENNEDY, 1963

In this chapter you will learn how to find and utilize the best investment research Web sites available on the Internet. Research is the foundation of successful investing. By the end of this chapter you will have the research skills needed to thoroughly research any investment before you buy or sell it.

Major investment firms such as Smith Barney and Merrill Lynch employ large staffs of financial analysts to scrutinize all facets of the financial world and the economy, including the health care industry, biotechnology, banking and finance, high-tech companies, retail sectors, heavy industry, transportation, recreation/entertainment, and the service economy. These experts use both technical and fundamental analyses to determine the inherent value of specific company stocks relative to other companies in a particular sector, as well as the performance of each industry group, in relation to the economy at large. Although this is not a perfect science, this research is invaluable in helping both professional advisors and individual investors make investment decisions. Here are the differences between fundamental and technical analysis.

Technical Analysis

Technical analysis attempts to detect and interpret patterns of a security primarily through the use of charts relating to price and volume. By carefully studying the cycles of a particular stock over many years, technical analysts hope to predict the future trend of an investment. They factor in daily fluctuations, as well as short- and long-term fluctuations. If it is true that history repeats itself, then these experts hope to reliably predict the supply and demand of a particular security or the markets. However, opponents of technical analysis believe that this approach does not take into account the overall direction of the entire stock market or the economy in general.

Fundamental Analysis

Fundamental analysis seeks to determine the intrinsic value of a given security by studying the fundamental economics of a company. Of course, many factors go into determining the value of a stock: current earnings, projected earnings, and dividends. Overhead has many factors to consider also: long-term debt, short-term debt, and the cost of goods and services. Once an intrinsic value of a stock is determined, this price is compared to the market price of the stock. If the stock is undervalued and there are no known risks involved, an analyst might recommend the stock as a "buy" or even "strong buy" depending on its future prospects. Fundamental analysis is by far the most common technique used by analysts and professional brokers. Many online sites offer fundamental research data on public companies traded on the major exchanges such as New York Stock Exchange and the NASDAQ.

> **Smart Investor Tip**
>
> Fundamental analysis works best when stocks are bought for the long haul. Most investments take time in order to reap the rewards of good research. Patience pays off.

Importance of Research Analysts

It is the duty of research analysts to keep brokers informed and up-to-date about new developments so they might better keep their clients' portfolios safe and profitable. Worldwide, it is estimated that billions of dollars are spent each year on research by investment brokers, bankers, financial planners, and individuals.

Prior to the Internet, the services and advice of these research analysts wasn't readily available to the individual investor without employing a full-service broker. By the time the research was made available to the general public via print media and television, the information was out of date and not as useful to the individual investor.

Today, the Internet has made it possible for the online investor to have real-time access to the same research that brokers have been privy to for years. Investors who feel comfortable surfing the World Wide Web and following up on the research links provided below will be in a much better position to make wise financial decisions. Many of the research sites are free, others charge a nominal fee. The following research sites require an investor to take the time to carefully study the wealth of information. Web sites on the Internet are improving and becoming more numerous by the minute. Even free government sites like the SEC's are now full of useful information for the online investor. Nowadays it is quite common for an investor to visit the Web site maintained by the very company that he is considering investing in.

Investors who don't feel comfortable researching investments on the Internet and interpreting the volume of information available are wise to employ the services of a full-service brokerage. Full-service brokers will interpret the research and make recommendations. There are Web sites that cater to novice or time-constrained investors. Several of these Web sites are so user-friendly they will track specific investments and alert you to news items pertaining to that investment. These sites can make portfolio tracking as simple as checking your appointment calendar.

Research Resources on the Internet

EDGAR's DATABASE (www.see.gov/edgarhp.htm)

The Securities and Exchange Commission requires publicly traded companies in the United States to register and file specific financial information. The SEC then makes this information available to the public via its EDGAR's database. EDGAR's database is a relatively simple but vital search engine. It permits you to search for a particular business by company name, date, ticker symbol, officers, industry, location, type of filing, or report number. EDGAR's database is one of the first Web sites investors should visit when considering investing in a company. EDGAR's database can let you know if the company actually exists and if all its filings are in order. Documents retrievable on EDGAR's that are of interest to the individual investor include:

Annual Reports

This report is the principle document issued by public companies to disclose corporate information to shareholders. It usually contains financial data, new products, research and development, market information, a letter from the CEO, and subsidiary activities.

Prospectus

This document contains basic financial information about a business with respect to security offerings.

Proxy Solicitation Materials

This document contains information about an upcoming vote. It is intended for shareholders that are entitled to vote.

1933 Registration Act Statements

This document is required of companies that are making a public offering. The document has two parts: a prospectus and registration information.

Investment Company Registration Statements

This form is required of investment companies offering mutual funds. It is a three-part form with a prospectus, additional financial information about the offering, and other required registration information. The information is intended to answer basic investor inquiries into the offering.

8-K Reports

This report must be filed when material events or corporate changes occur that may be of consequence to investors. This includes events such as mergers or acquisitions. The report must be filed within ten days of such an event.

10-K Report

This report is an annual report that companies file annually with the SEC. It gives a comprehensive overview of a company's business dealings for the year.

S-1 Reports

This report is required when a company makes an initial public offering (IPO).

S-3 Reports

This report is filed when secondary stock is offered to the public.

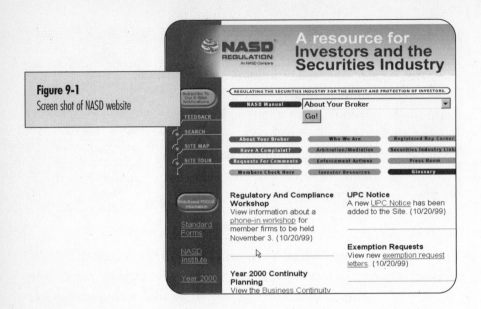

Figure 9-1
Screen shot of NASD website

FYI

Security brokers and public companies are regulated and licensed in the state where they are headquartered. Questions about a broker or a company can frequently be answered at a Web site maintained by the state it is located in.

NASD (www.nasdr.com)

The National Association of Security Dealers regulates brokers in the United States. They set the laws and guidelines by which all security brokers in the United States must operate. They regularly issue warnings about brokers whose licenses have been suspended. They are also doing their best to monitor and upgrade the quality of Internet trading. This site is informative and user-friendly to the investing public as well as to brokers. Complaints against brokers or companies may be issued online at this site.

Company and Industry Web Sites

Most major corporations now maintain a Web site for customers, wholesalers, and investors. Keep in mind that these Web sites are often designed and maintained by professional webmasters who know how to make a Web site very appealing. Many of these Web sites invite the potential investor to view the company's goods, services, and annual report and to invest in the company.

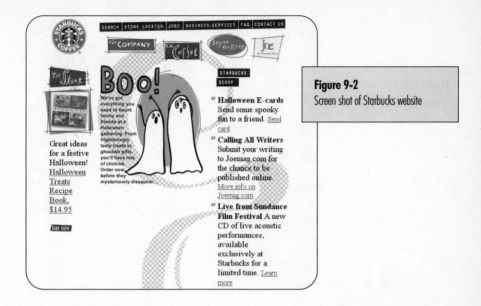

Figure 9-2
Screen shot of Starbucks website

Newsgroups

For the investor with the time, useful financial information can be found at newsgroups. Newsgroups are essentially personal letters, commentaries, and responses Internet users leave on a database. The range of topics at newsgroups is quite wide and varied. The downloading of programs or information found at questionable newsgroups is to be avoided for fear of encountering a computer virus or illicit material. A good search engine is necessary to find a newsgroup of financial interest to you. Many of the postings are about personal encounters with companies or products. The postings can be quite animated and intense, and further research should be done to verify statements found at newsgroups.

You can post messages or questions yourself, and the outpouring of responses may overwhelm you because the entire World Wide Web may very well read and respond to your posting. The following search engine should help narrow your search for worthwhile newsgroups.

Time Out

A visit to the Web site of a company can be extremely informative. Remember that these Web sites are essentially advertisements, and the investment potential of the company may be exaggerated.

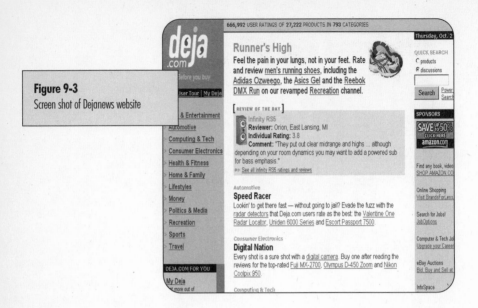

Figure 9-3
Screen shot of Dejanews website

DejaNews (www.dejanews.com)

This site will seek out finance-related newsgroups for you. The search engine can track newsgroups by subject, author, group or date. Once you find an appropriate newsgroup you can join the newsgroup or bookmark it for easy revisiting.

Independent Consumer Information Sites

Wise investors use the services of online, independent research firms. Investment research gathered at corporate and government Web sites can leave an investor feeling unsure about an investment. Independent research firms gather essential data about a particular investment and present it in a coherent and objective fashion. Known facts about a company are prioritized and collated in such a way that investors can make a knowledgeable and unbiased decision about a company's investment potential. Most of these firms have been in business long before the Internet.

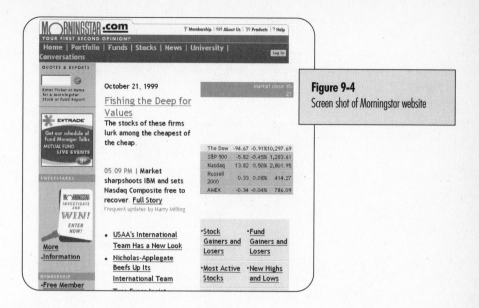

Figure 9-4
Screen shot of Morningstar website

MORNINGSTAR (www.morningstar.com)

This independent research and rating company is a favorite among financial professionals. Their specialty is mutual funds, but other financial information is available online. Morningstar features an easy-to-use search engine that hastens your search for a worthwhile investment. The site also carries feature articles as well as useful research links.

MOODY'S (www.moody's.com)

Moody's is best known as an established bond rating company. It assigns a rating to bonds by taking into account such factors as past earnings, future earnings, management, financial worthiness, and the nature of the business. This site takes some of the fear out of shopping for quality bonds.

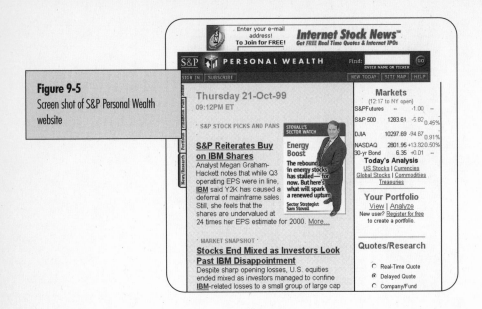

Figure 9-5
Screen shot of S&P Personal Wealth
website

S&P PERSONAL WEALTH (www.personalwealth.com)

With a subscription, this site offers advice for the individual investor. The professional investor or broker will find more in-depth articles on investments and companies at S&P Advisor Insight *www.advisorinsight.com*.

NEWSPAPERS

Up-to-date financial news is available at Web sites maintained by newspapers. The financial news at these sites is more convenient, and timelier, than hard copy editions. The better newspapers include delayed time stock quotes, limited research capabilities, and portfolio management.

WALL STREET JOURNAL (www.wsj.com)

This site offers two levels of service: free and fee-based. Paid subscribers have access to portfolio management, late-breaking news, stock tables, press releases, and excellent links to other financial resources. Market alerts can automatically be sent to your e-mail address.

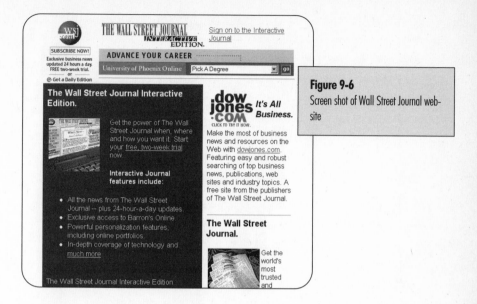

Figure 9-6
Screen shot of Wall Street Journal website

NEW YORK TIMES (www.nytimes.com)

This site is an excellent source for financial news and features, as well as stock quotes. The online edition of the *New York Times* gives access to a portfolio tracker.

INVESTOR'S BUSINESS DAILY (www.investors.com)

This site is a good resource for the novice as well as the savvy investor. The news presented here is considered by many investors to be objective and useful. On-site educational material is available.

FINANCIAL TIMES (www.ft.com)

This site offers timely world financial news as well as in-depth reports on all segments of the economy.

Figure 9-7
Screen shot of Invest-O-Rama website

Newsletters

Several thousand financial newsletters are available online. Many are free and can be read online or delivered directly to your e-mail address. Be careful to register with only select newsletters pertinent to your financial investments, otherwise your e-mail mailbox may be swamped with responses. Many of these newsletters are actually advertisements for investments, and further investigation is essential to avoid unscrupulous investment scams. The wealth of information available in newsletters is so immense that it is wise to use a directory that outlines what information is contained in the newsletter. There are several Web sites that search out newsletters of specific interest to you:

Helpful Hint

Most full editions of an online magazine cost money, but limited editions are generally free. Guest subscriptions are usually available for investors who want to check out a magazine before subscribing.

Newsletter Access: Investments
    www.newsletteraccess.com
InvestorGuide *www.investorguide.com*
GS Research on Demand *www.gsnews.com*
Holt Stock Report *www.metro.turnpike.net/holt*
Kiplinger Online *www.kiplinger.com*
Invest-O-Rama *www.investorama.com*

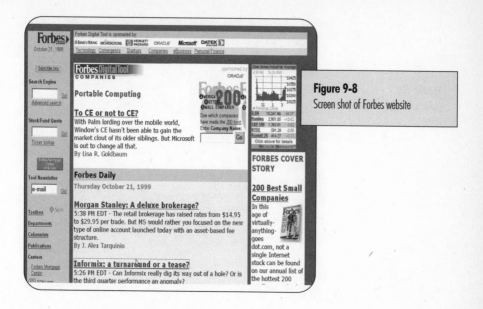

Figure 9-8
Screen shot of Forbes website

Online Magazines

Full versions of the best financial magazines are now available online for a subscription fee. Not only is the reading of financial magazines and newspapers online an ecologically sound practice (fewer trees are cut), the online versions are more up-to-date than hard copy versions. Most magazines specialize in entertaining and educational feature stories of interest to a wide range of investors.

FORBES (www.forbes.com)

The online edition of *Forbes* has many features to assist the wise investor.

BARRONS ONLINE (www.barrons.com)

A limited edition of this well-respected magazine is available for free. The full edition, with archival access, Market Lab, and Weekday Extra, is available for a fee.

FORTUNE (www.pathfinder.com)

This popular Web site has well-written feature articles and reports as well as quotes. A portfolio planner can track investments.

Figure 9-9
Screen shot of Mutual Funds Online website

MUTUAL FUNDS ONLINE (www.mfmag.com)

This site has many free links to useful financial services and information. A paid subscription provides the subscriber with the full contents of the magazine and archival files.

KIPLINGER ONLINE (www.kiplinger.com)

This powerful Web site provides subscribers with access to a wide range of financial information and advice. The site caters to personal financial planning and assistance.

Search Engine Web Sites

To effectively research investments on the Internet you first and foremost must find a search engine that you feel comfortable with. Search engines have come a long way in the last few years, and good ones are amazingly efficient at finding the information you need in a hurry. Most major search engines have added financial links to their home pages, and they are becoming more sophisticated all the time. You will need to test the effectiveness of different search engines before settling with one. Also, depending on the characteristics of your portfolio, you may find that three

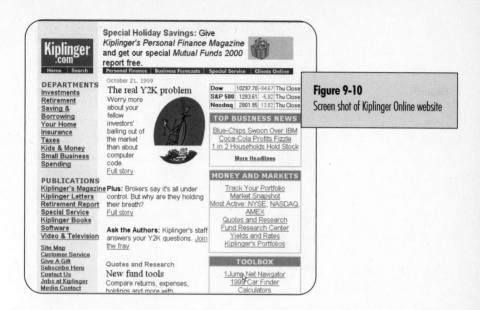

Figure 9-10
Screen shot of Kiplinger Online website

or four different search engines are required to effectively track and research your investments. The list of possible search engines is immense, but here are a few popular ones:

Yahoo! *www.yahoo.com*
Dogpile *www.dogpile.com*
Alta Vista *www.altavista.com*
Excite *www.excite.com*
Infoseek *www.infoseek.com*

Characteristics of a Good Search Engine

The search engine should not smother you with advertisements that distract you from the work at hand. If necessary, find a search engine that doesn't obliterate your screen with advertisements.

- A good search engine should have an intensive search function, which saves you from wading through page after page of possible hits. The intensive search should find a Web site according to exact wording, date, and name or subject.

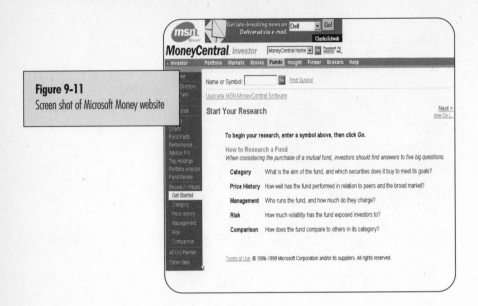

Figure 9-11
Screen shot of Microsoft Money website

- A good search engine has links that are pertinent to your interests. If the search engine seems to be a good starting point for research, bookmark it or make it your home page.
- A good search engine provides free e-mail capabilities. It is a good idea to maintain more than one e-mail address. I use one address for personal and important correspondence and another address for less important and less time-sensitive correspondence.

ALTA VISTA (www.altavista.com)

Alta Vista is an excellent all-purpose search engine that has been around for years. Its database covers a wide array of topics and it has an intensive search function. Many reference librarians use Alta Vista because of its access to huge databases.

MICROSOFT MONEY (www.investor.msn.com)

This search engine has grown by leaps and bounds in the last few years. It has affiliations with major news organizations and software firms. Be assured that this Web site will improve on a daily basis. E-mail is free here via Hotmail.

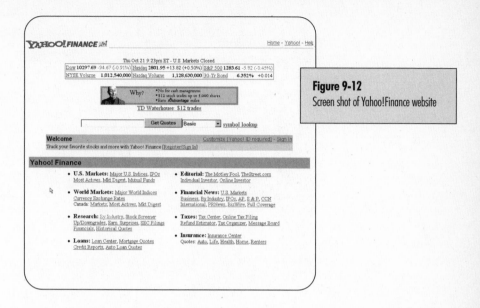

Figure 9-12
Screen shot of Yahoo!Finance website

YAHOO!FINANCE (www.yahoo.com)

Yahoo!Finance is a fast and effective search engine with an excellent search function that speeds you through the research process. The Yahoo!Finance portal has excellent research capabilities and deserves a walk through. As we follow the steps necessary to research a stock you will notice there are links that we could have followed depending on the stock or the goal of our research. To fully research an investment it is wise to follow all possible links. With Yahoo!Finance as our search engine we will research the Disney Company, which has the ticker symbol "DIS."

The first screen we see when clicking on Yahoo!Finance is relatively self-explanatory; it breaks the economy into major categories, and within each segment of the economy we see that each segment is broken down further. Our choice, Disney, demands that we click on Entertainment under the heading Recreation/Entertainment. Next we type in the ticker symbol for the Disney Company and highlight "profile."

The profile of the company gives an excellent snapshot of a company. The officers are listed and a brief business summary follows. If we have questions about, for example, the loss of $159 million dollars in the equity of Infoseek, we will want to click on investor relations or company

Figure 9-13
Screen shot of Stock Tables of Yahoo!Finance

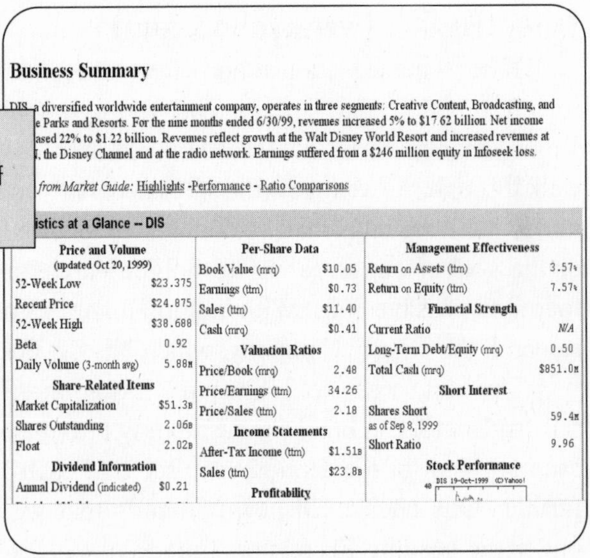

Figure 9-14
Screen shot of Yahoo!Finance Profile of Walt Disney Company

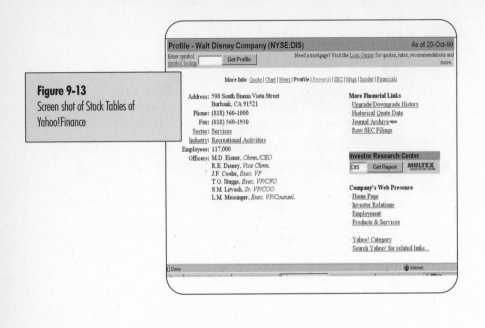

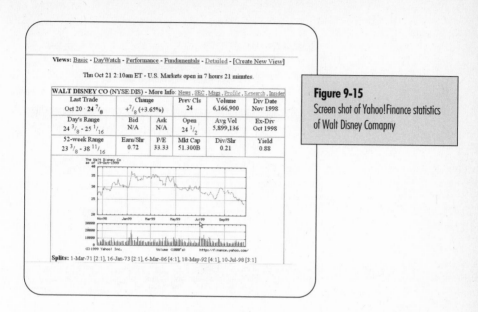

Figure 9-15
Screen shot of Yahoo!Finance statistics of Walt Disney Comapny

research until we find the information we are looking for. We must follow all research links until this question or any others are fully explained to our satisfaction before we invest in the company.

Under Statistics at a Glance we can learn a great deal about the performance of the Walt Disney Company. We learn that the recent price of Disney stock is near its 52 week low. We also see that with a beta of 0.92 Disney is considered a fairly safe investment.

Clicking on the research button reading left to right, we see the symbol for Disney is "DIS" followed by the time the last trade of Disney stock was posted. In this posting, we learn the stock market has closed.

The next box tells what the change for the day was. Under volume we learn how many shares of Disney stock were traded on this day. If the number of shares traded for the day is exceptionally high, we should do further research into why.

At the bottom of the chart we might want to click on recent news concerning the Walt Disney company. Recent new can have a good, bad, or trivial effect on the stock price. We know that a high-profile company like Disney is always making

> **Just a Reminder**
>
> Time is of the essence in stock trading.

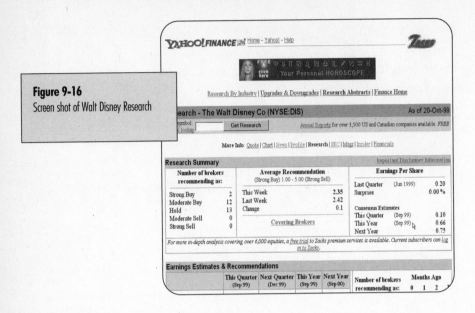

Figure 9-16
Screen shot of Walt Disney Research

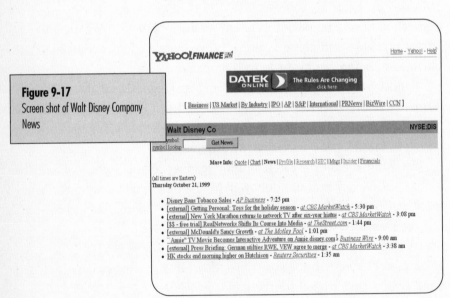

Figure 9-17
Screen shot of Walt Disney Company News

the news whether it is a lawsuit from an injured visitor to one of their theme parks or a management shuffle. Significant news about a company like Disney usually causes a fluctuation in the price of its stock.

You now have the major tools necessary to make sound investment choices right at your fingertips. However, like all tools, you must know how to use them. This will require some time and practice. Have patience with yourself and the learning process. It will pay off.

Smart Investor Tip

Before buying or selling any stock, do your research and make sure you've taken into account the latest news about the company. It could either make or save you money.

CHAPTER TEN

Smart Tools Available Online

Man is a tool using animal . . . Without tools he is nothing, with tools he is all.

—THOMAS CARLYLE, 1776

This chapter will expand on the research skills learned in the previous chapter. The Internet is packed with more investment tools than one person could possibly use in a lifetime. To help make your tool search easier, you'll find some of the most user-friendly, reliable tools outlined in this chapter. The more advanced you become in your knowledge and skill level, the more fun you'll have experimenting with the more sophisticated tools and Web sites.

It was only a few years ago that the typical investor checked the performance of his investments by tuning the television to the six o'clock news and seeing what the Dow Jones Industrial Average did for the day. The typical investor assumed his investments did roughly about the same as the Dow. Hopefully, he thought, as he glanced at a three-day-old *Wall Street Journal*, "My broker will notify me if something dramatic happens." When he got really nervous about the stock market, he would visit his broker's office at lunchtime to watch the stock symbols tick by. Today, unfortunately, the skills of many investors haven't advanced much beyond this.

The reasons are many and varied:

"I don't feel secure using a computer to track my own portfolio."

"I'm overwhelmed by the choices."

"I keep getting distracted by the advertisements and the hype."

"I can't comprehend the charts and graphs."

All these excuses and more are valid. Online trading is brand new to everyone, including the brokers. Hundreds of investor Web sites are coming online daily. Existing Web sites are adding new features and appearances. Insecurity about online trading is a normal response to the fast paced, ever changing world of the Internet.

However, there is a solution to Internet insecurity. Ironically, the solution itself is to be found in cyberspace. The novice online trader must remain calm and patient while learning the tools needed to safely navigate towards profitable online trading. In this chapter you will maneuver from Web site to Web site, progressively learning to utilize software programs that will teach you to make appropriate financial decisions. You will learn to:

A. Practice online investing with play money, as you did with *Monopoly*® as a child.

B. Learn to use calculators that automatically compute complex financial equations.

C. Find the right stock at the right price with stock screening software.

D. Read graphs and charts that previously looked like lines on a seismograph.

E. Learn about hot IPO's before they are offered.

F. Plan your financial future in the comfort of your home.

Learning Tools

One of the major reasons why investors don't manage their finances online is they find the Internet with all of its choices overwhelming. Which broker should I sign with? Is it safe? Which software program is right for me? What's a stop limit order? Thankfully, public agencies and private businesses have heard investor's pleas for help. Now hundreds of Internet sites are devoted to teaching investors the skills necessary to manage their money online.

Helpful Online Consumer Sites

SECURITIES AND EXCHANGE COMMISSION (www.sec.gov./oieal.htm)

The SEC is very concerned about the impact the Internet has on investing. They are to be commended for quickly recognizing problems and maintaining a Web site warning investors and brokers about the potential pitfalls of online investing. The SEC hopes to alleviate some of the problems by providing valuable links to investor education material. One link leads you to online publications that teach the basics of investing. Another link connects to sites that introduce you to the Internet and online trading. There is also a link to interactive tools for investors. The SEC site, as already mentioned, provides a search engine that retrieves articles of interest to the beginning investor from its EDGAR database.

AMERICAN ASSOCIATION OF RETIRED PERSONS (www.aarp.org)

AARP is a well-respected organization that zealously protects the well-being of retired persons. Their Web site is extremely helpful to novice investors of any age. AARP is especially concerned about fraudulent investing schemes perpetrated against elderly persons over the Internet.

AMERICAN ASSOCIATION OF INDIVIDUAL INVESTORS (www.aaii.com)

AAII is a nonprofit organization established in 1978. Its 175,000 members receive a copy of the *AAII Journal*, which focuses on the basics of investing. Their Web site is extremely helpful for the online trader. Their downloadable library contains five files that teach the basics of investing. They include Investment Basics Video Clip, Mutual Fundamentals, Commission Schedules, Financial Competence, and Portfolio Management. They offer a free two-week trial membership, after which the annual dues are $49, which includes a subscription to the *AAII Journal*.

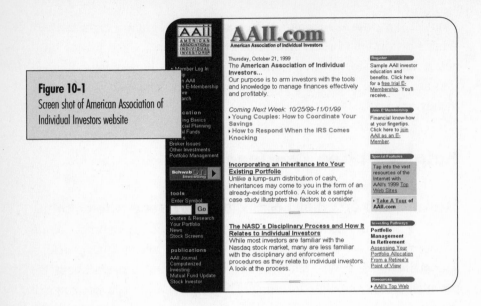

Figure 10-1
Screen shot of American Association of Individual Investors website

INVESTORGUIDE (www.investorguide.com)

The comprehensive list of research links at this site make it a likely candidate for a bookmark or homepage because the easier an important financial link is to find, the more likely you'll visit it. This Web site partitions financial links into three major categories: investing, personal finance, and learning.

The investing links direct you to sites specializing in news, stocks, quotes, market summary, public company directory, EDGAR SEC filings, historical data, IPOs, mutual funds, fund research, fund list, brokers, online trading, international investing, exchanges, investing in net stocks, and DRIPs.

Personal finance links feature sites on car buying, home buying, college, retirement, Roth IRA, loans, credit, insurance, banking, taxes, advisors, kids and money, books, magazines, software, and electronic commerce.

Learning links direct you to sites on investment clubs, principles of investing, overall strategy, analysis form, pros, calculators, portfolio tracking, and contests.

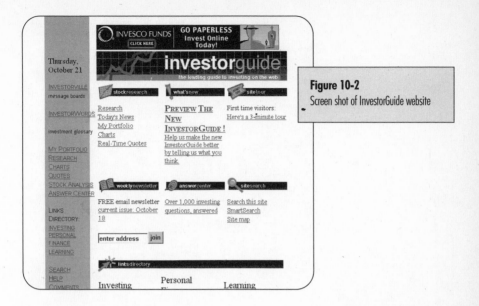

Figure 10-2
Screen shot of InvestorGuide website

Interactive Games

The novice investor is advised to take advantage of the numerous Web sites offering free access to interactive games that teach the basics of investing. The interactive games are created for fun and learning. The themes of the games, sure to be of interest to a wide variety of investors, include sports, music, movies, and even Wall Street. Most interactive games provide you with "funny money" to play with, up to $100,000 at many sites. Your job is to wisely invest and try to show a profit despite sometimes bizarre market conditions and fluctuations. Some interactive game sites charge to participate but offer challengers a cash reward if they win the game.

FYI

Free interactive game sites often have sponsors or advertisers from the financial world. The names of these advertisers frequently appear on screen with links to their Web sites. It is best to avoid the come-ons of these ads unless you want to be bombarded by e-mail.

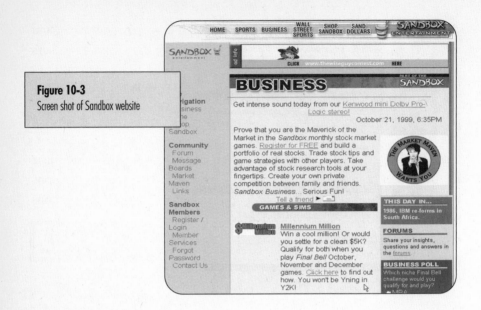

Figure 10-3
Screen shot of Sandbox website

FINAL BELL (www.sandbox.com)

Final Bell is a sophisticated interactive game in which Wall Street realistically determines the outcome. Players are allotted $100,000 to start play. The player with the most money after one month wins a cash prize, usually a few hundred dollars. At all times during trading players have ready access to a stock symbol directory, big board statistics, stock quotes, and charts. When a player feels ready to invest real money on Wall Street, a direct link to major brokerage houses is just a mouse click away. Research will have to been done elsewhere, or through the brokerage links, because links to research sites were not present at press time.

YAHOO! INVESTMENT CHALLENGE (www.yahoo.com)

This interactive game is free to those who register. One hundred thousand dollars is yours to start the game! You are welcome to invest as you see fit. The object is to show the most profit at end of play. The power of Yahoo!'s financial research engine is at the player's fingertips during play.

VIRTUAL STOCK EXCHANGE (www.virtualstockexchange.com)

This fun site offers free competition while learning the ins and outs of the stock market. The Web site claims to have 60,000 players. It has dozens of actual links to research, advice, chat rooms, software, and more. The site also offers a link to teaching aids for high school teachers and college professors.

Online Calculators

Online calculators are no longer simple numerical keypads for basic mathematical calculations. Today they quickly answer financial questions that previously took an accountant hours to compute. Complex questions such as, If I need x amount of dollars per month in retirement income, how much should I be saving per month now? What is my net worth? How much capital gains tax do I owe on the profits from my sale of stock? How much will I get from Social Security when I retire? How much of my assets should I keep liquid for emergencies? The answers to these questions and more can be easily found online.

> **Helpful Hint**
>
> Most topnotch calculators are available online for free. Web sites often offer these calculators as an enticement for you to visit their site. Financial institutions and stockbrokers offer free calculators because they hope you discover that you have expendable income or assets that you can invest with them. Government and nonprofit organizations offer calculators as a public service.

For the most part, the calculators offered online are easy to use and only require you to fill in the blank spaces. You need not have a mathematical mind or be computer savvy. However, you should be prepared to furnish the calculators with basic personal and financial information about yourself and your family: your income, your expenses, your assets, your long-term debt, your age, and your financial goals. The more complex the calculator, the more blanks you will have to fill in. Once the questionnaire is complete the calculator does the computations. There are calculators to assess your risk level, determine if your are an aggressive or conservative investor, recommend a savings or investment plan, and even tell you if you aren't in a financial position to invest anything. If the calculator at a brokerage house determines that you would make an excellent online investor, you will, naturally, be invited to interact further and invest with the firm.

KIPLINGER'S CALCULATORS (www.kiplinger.com)

Kiplinger's magazine has a well-designed Web site that offers ten user-friendly calculator programs. The free calculators at the Web site include:

1. A calculator that caters to children and money. It will figure the cost of college or the total cost of raising a child from infancy to adulthood.
2. A spending calculator that determines the actual cost of major purchases including car loans at different interest rates.
3. A saving and borrowing calculator that figures the financial rewards of various savings plans and the true cost of borrowing money.
4. A tax calculator that estimates your income, property, and social security tax.
5. An insurance calculator that calculates mortgage insurance costs based on the amount of your home loan. This calculator will also figure the cost of life insurance and how much coverage you should carry based on the personal data you enter.
6. A calculator to figure the cost of home ownership, including the total interest paid, fifteen- versus thirty-year mortgages, refinance charges, closing costs, benefits of extra payments, and the best mortgage brokers.
7. A stock calculator that computes profit or loss at specified market conditions.
8. A mutual fund calculator.
9. An investment calculator that calculates various investment plans and their rewards.
10. A retirement planner that helps you plan your retirement strategy.

The investor is cautioned not to rely entirely on the answers or figures that various calculators present. First of all, calculators, like computers, are only as reliable as the data programmed into them. More often than not there are extenuating circumstances surrounding every investor's portfolio, variables such as personality, a death in the family, unexpected depreciation of assets, or an inheritance. Always research an investment to the best of your ability, and if you still have questions and doubts about the

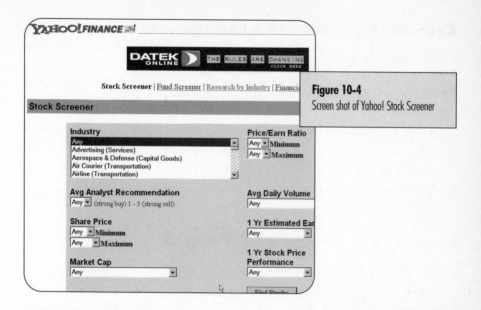

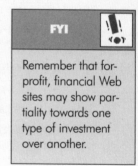

Figure 10-4
Screen shot of Yahoo! Stock Screener

integrity of the investment, seek the advice of a financial professional and conduct further research. Because calculators are so accessible on the Internet, it is also advisable to try the same calculation with another calculator at a different Web site. Interesting point: these calculators often come up with diverse answers or solutions because they are programmed to interpret data differently.

> **FYI**
>
> Remember that for-profit, financial Web sites may show partiality towards one type of investment over another.

Stock Screening Tools

Stock screening programs help you choose a stock that fits exactly your investor profile and goals. The screening of stocks is accomplished by software that is capable of searching through volumes of stock information according to parameters that you set. Free and fee-based screening programs all work basically the same way. You are asked for a set of characteristics or variables that you want a stock to possess, and then it retrieves the stock, or stocks, for you. If your preferences are not well defined the search may return a hundred stocks. By fine tuning the preferences you desire in a stock you will narrow

Helpful Hint

The variables that a stock screening program searches for can number anywhere from ten to 400. Use these programs to search for a variety of options simultaneously.

the choices down to a half dozen. Further research may be necessary to narrow the list down to one stock.

The fee-based Web site of the American Association of Individual Investor *www.aaii.com* has an extensive database with sophisticated screening software. Investors will delight in the ability of the software to narrow down stock choices.

Investment Charts and Graphs

Charts and graphs are readily available on the Internet for free. Full-service brokers usually include access to charts and graphs as a part of their service or commission charge. Whichever financial Web site you refer to often should have the ability to display charts and graphs because complex statistics about a company can be made comprehensible when displayed as a chart or graph. The chart and graph software that you choose should offer the following features and options:

- The ability to call up performance data by the day, week, quarter, year, and historically.
- Easy to read and resizable to fit your screen.
- The ability to be displayed in different formats such as a spreadsheet or text file.
- Further research options at the click of a mouse.

Financial Planning Software

Investors have three alternatives when choosing software that tracks and manages their portfolios. The price of some of the software can be relatively high when purchasing top of the line portfolio management software, which, however, usually comes bundled with other financial software programs.

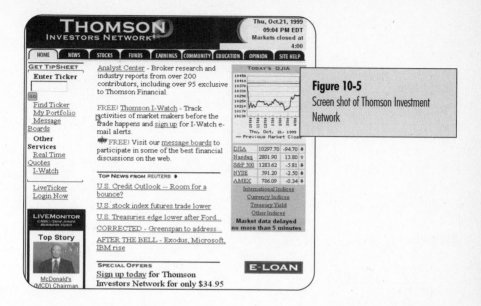

Figure 10-5
Screen shot of Thomson Investment Network

OWNER/USER SOFTWARE

These programs can be installed directly into the hard drive of your computer. Although these portfolio management software programs can be quite pricey, up to $500, the more expensive programs come with added features and options that can be essential to serious minded investors. These software packages frequently are bundled with retirement, college, and tax planning programs. Online banking software is also included with many software packages, which allow the user to accomplish all his or her banking needs from a home PC. Built-in calculators compute the data that you enter.

> **Helpful Hint**
>
> Investors with little patience or skill for understanding software are wise to use the portfolio management software available at full-service brokers.

QUICKEN 99 (www.quicken99.com)

This well-respected software company offers complete financial management packages for the individual investor. Once this software is installed on your hard drive you can do all your banking at home. "Investment Tools" will manage your portfolio expertly. The add-on

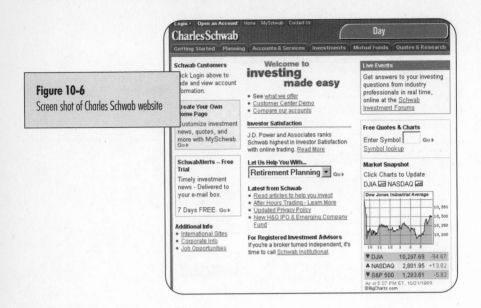

Figure 10-6
Screen shot of Charles Schwab website

financial programs will make you think an accountant, a banker, a financial planner, and a stockbroker live inside your computer.

BROKERAGE SOFTWARE

Full-service brokers usually include sophisticated portfolio management software as part of their monthly fee. This usually includes automatic updating of your portfolio. The investor has access twenty-four hours a day to the portfolio's net worth, asset allocation, order status, cash balances, margin balances, and an activity report. A full-service broker can usually send notification of important portfolio activity by e-mail or voicemail, depending on urgency.

Charles Schwab (www.schwab.com)

This firm has adapted to online trading like a duck to a pond. They offer complete portfolio management as part of their commission, as well as many levels of service.

Merrill Lynch (www.mlonline.com)

The largest full-service investment company in the world has an online site that will give you a chance to compare both cost and services.

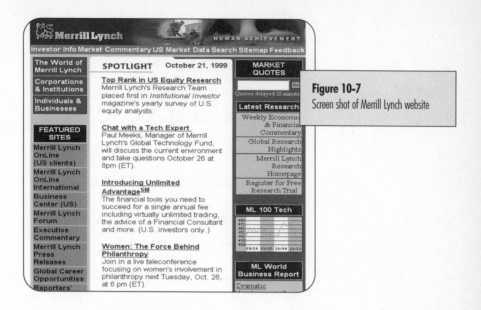

Figure 10-7
Screen shot of Merrill Lynch website

Their interactive platform for online trading is due to launch in December, 1999.

INTERNET ACCESSIBLE SOFTWARE

Many financial sites on the Web offer free access to basic portfolio management software. Even major search engines such as Yahoo! Finance and Microsoft's MSN Investor contain portfolio management software. Most deep discount and discount brokerages also offer the use of portfolio tracking software. Much of it is free and easy to use. However, with most free portfolio management software found on the Internet the investor may have to manually update the portfolio with new investment data, whereas at a full-service broker updating and notification of changes are completed for you.

The New York Times (www.nytimes.com)

This online news site offers free use of their portfolio management software. The quotes are updated periodically and financial news is just a click away at this site.

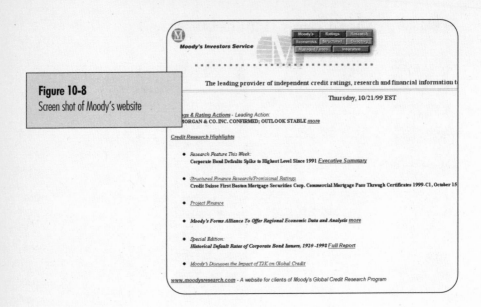

Figure 10-8
Screen shot of Moody's website

Bond Tracking Programs

Many previously mentioned financial Web sites also offer information about various types of bonds, including price histories, yields, ratings, recent issues, and news. However, there are a few Web sites that specialize in the bond market, and the wise online trader will research these Web sites before making an investment in bonds.

MOODY'S (www.moods.com)

John Moody founded the company in 1909 when he saw a need for safe investments in the railroads. Obviously, he made good investment decisions because the company survived the Great Depression. Today, the company's Web site is a good place to research bonds. A search engine is readily available that easily tracks bonds according to rating and type: corporate, utility, industrial, or government. Moody's clearly explains their rating system in concise terms that takes the fear out of investing in bonds. A great deal of financial security can be derived from following the many research links provided at this site.

STANDARD & POOR'S (www.standardpoor.com)

This company is an internationally known and highly respected credit rating service. They assess all types of bond issues and their ratings are highly regarded by both individual and institutional investors.

Tracking Tools for Initial Public Offerings and Direct Public Offerings

The risky and time-sensitive nature of trading in initial public offerings (IPO) and direct public offerings (DPO) requires the prudent investor to use research tools specifically designed to locate and research them. Fortunately, the recent publicity surrounding "hot" Internet related IPOs has spawned numerous Web sites that specialize in IPO and DPO tracking and research. Although a trader can, and should, research an IPO and DPO at the SEC's EDGAR database, much more intensive research can be done at specialized sites.

The pros of cons of the IPO must be fully researched. Remember: many IPO's don't go "hot" their first day out, and others are "hot" for only a few days. Read comments about what the experts think the holding period for the stock should be. It is amazing how many IPO offerings are for companies that have never shown a profit and, in all likelihood, may never show a profit. A good research site will inform you if well-respected underwriters endorse the IPO or DPO. The Web site should inform you who is involved in the underwriting of the company and, if so, the firm's rate of success. The Web site should fully explain the prospects for future business. If it's a high-tech IPO, is the product definitely in demand? Is there any competition? If you are naïve about the high-tech industry, consider investing in a business with goods or services you

FYI

IPO research sites should contain the preliminary prospectus that is filed with the SEC. The site should also contain pertinent information about the company's management team, including their experience and success rate. The site should also give a detailed explanation of what the business intends to accomplish with the influx of investment capital. The site should furnish advice from financial professionals regarding the IPO.

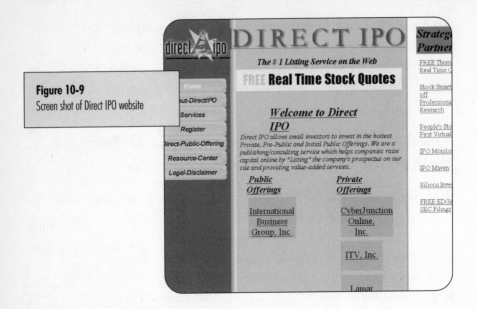

Figure 10-9
Screen shot of Direct IPO website

more fully understand. Don't get caught in the gambling fever that accompanies many IPOs and DPOs.

DIRECT IPO (www.directipo.com)

This Web site specializes in researching IPOs and DPOs of high-tech and Internet stocks, and they do it well. They have a link to a glossary of words commonly used in this niche of the financial world. They also provide access to archival files and to SEC filings.

HOOVER'S ONLINE (www.ipodirect.com)

This Web site is a must for novice IPO investors. It provides learning materials and a tour of the site. There are direct links to late breaking news items at financial publications, including the *Wall Street Journal*, *New York Times*, *Bloomberg*, and the Dow Jones Publication Library.

Glossaries

Financial Web sites have responded to the growing need for online financial glossaries and dictionaries. It is too expensive and time consuming to refer to a hard copy financial dictionary every time you're unsure of the meaning of a word. Today, many Web sites are conveniently placing a direct link to a glossary. The melding of computer language and financial lingo and the influx of new investors is responsible for the strong demand for up-to-date glossaries. Even longstanding brokers admit to looking up words such as "cookie." Free financial glossaries and dictionaries are to be found at many Web sites. If a glossary isn't available on screen, it is a good idea to bookmark a glossary for quick reference when the need arises.

Yahoo! Finance (www.finance.yahoo.com)

This site has a powerful, complete glossary. The glossary is so huge that it is almost unwieldy; the viewer must click on the link to the first letter of the desired word and then scroll down to the exact word.

New York Stock Exchange (www.nyse.com)

The NYSE provides an online glossary of terms and acronyms to assist traders and brokers with words frequently used on Wall Street. The glossary is concise and complete in its definition of complex words and phrases. All twenty-four pages of the glossary are downloadable.

Time Saver

If you don't want to look up a word or financial term online, just skip to the back of this book. We've included a comprehensive glossary here for your convenience.

Options and Futures Dictionary (www.cme.com/market/glossary.html)

The Chicago Mercantile Exchange maintains this Web page. It is a small glossary that focuses on words commodity traders use in their very specialized marketplace. The glossary has direct links to more detailed explanations of complex words and concepts.

Investor Words (www.investorwords.com)

This site claims to have the most comprehensive financial glossary anywhere. It contains 5,000 definitions and 15,000 links between related terms. It is managed by InvestorGuide.com, Inc. which, as mentioned previously, is an excellent financial site with many great links.

CHAPTER ELEVEN

Fool's Gold: A Word of Caution

Experience keeps a dear school, but fools will learn in no other.
—BENJAMIN FRANKLIN, *POOR RICHARD'S ALMANACK*, 1743

In this chapter you will learn how to recognize and avoid potential online investment scams, which have become rampant on the Internet. You will learn what to look for, how to conduct your own investigation on investment tips, and how not to get swindled by scams.

During the California gold rush, unscrupulous men would often sell worthless mines and gold claims to naïve miners. They would point to the numerous shiny specks of gold-colored objects in the water and tell the miners that the area was laden with gold. Believing they had hit pay dirt, the unsuspecting miners would pay top dollar for these mine claims. After days of panning, the miners would take their discoveries to the local weigh master only to be told that what they owned was "fool's gold," or iron pyrite.

Today, a new breed of unscrupulous individuals is using the Internet to pawn worthless schemes. Amazingly, worthless gold mines (along with dozens of other fraudulent schemes) are still being peddled. Every day one Ponzi scheme or another rips someone off. Generally speaking (for some reason that I've never quite grasped), people are easily drawn into the excitement and possibility of "get rich quick" schemes. It does not seem to matter that most of these deals come with red flags and neon signs blinking "stop, don't do it." People do it anyway. And they lose money. Sometimes they lose their money, their house and the shirt off their back. I do not want anyone who reads this book to ever have that experience, so pay attention.

Investment fraud is at an all time high. The government has created a special task force in an attempt to help reduce this problem. However, the Internet, due to its dynamic, fast-paced nature, has created an enormous opportunity for techno thieves. The Securities and Exchange Commission created its first nationwide operation, called "Internet Sweep," in October of 1998 in an effort to combat Internet fraud. As a result of these efforts, many enforcement actions have been taken against individuals and companies in connection with Internet fraud crimes committed against investors around the world.

Helpful Hint

The Securities and Exchange Commission's Web Site www.sec.gov offers helpful advice regarding how to avoid online investment scams and gives detailed information on some of the most recent litigation. This should be required reading because these cases clearly demonstrate how sophisticated some of these scams are and how many people they have affected.

On February 25, 1999, the SEC released the results of actions taken against thirteen individuals and companies across the country. These cases involved a variety of illegal practices including fraudulent spam mail (Internet junk mail), online newsletters, online message board postings, and Web site fraud. In most of the cases the individuals and companies were found to have misrepresented information about companies or failed to disclose the nature, source, and compensation received for their advertising services. According to the SEC press release, over $450,000 in cash and approximately 2.7 million shares of stocks and options were paid to fraudulent Internet scams.

Not all of these scams occur on the Internet, however. Some of them are set up as "boiler-room" operations, or makeshift business fronts conducted largely over the phone. Generally, there is no legitimate business, no investment "opportunity," and the operation will have taken the money and run within a short period of time.

Industry Cold Call Rules

Cold calls from people who are licensed to sell securities are required to be conducted in a certain manner. The securities industry has been cold calling potential customers since the beginning of time, and they are generally professional and polite. Not everyone calling you is a scam artist. Many of these brokers are from reputable brokerage houses or regional firms and are honest people trying to make a living. They often have good advice and ideas to offer. These are the rules they are required to follow and usually do:

- Call only between 8:00 A.M. and 9:00 P.M.
- Say who they are and why they are calling.
- Give you their firm's name, location, and phone number.
- Tell you the purpose of their call.
- Put you on their "do not call list" if you ask them not to call back.
- Treat you with respect.
- Tell you the truth. If someone lies to you regarding any aspect of an investment, they are in violation of both federal and state securities laws.

Time Saver

All major brokerage firms have a "do not call" list that they must keep on file. If you do not wish to be cold called, you can request that your name be added to this list.

Here are some of the telltale signs of an investment scam cold call:

1. The caller offers inside information. In this case you should just hang up. If you have caller ID, take down the number and contact the SEC.
2. The salesperson pressures you to make a quick decision. This is meant to prevent you from properly investigating the company.
3. The salesperson is offering an unusually high return on your money and/or outrageous profits.
4. The profits are "guaranteed." (Big red flag on this one.)
5. The investment is touted as a "once-in-a-lifetime" opportunity and is available for a limited time only. This is not a lie. It is a

once-in-lifetime opportunity to go broke, and you do have to do it soon because this guy has plans to be in the Bahamas with your money by next week.

6. The salesperson tells you the investment is "risk free." There is no such thing as a risk-free investment unless it's in an insured product such as a certificate of deposit or insured bond.

7. When you ask for written information, you never receive it or it is given reluctantly.

8. If the promoters are using an alias or pseudonym there is a strong possibility they are trying to hide their true identity.

9. Offshore investment opportunities (or any investment outside the United States) are problematic for any investor. If something does go wrong, which happens too frequently, it is difficult to even find out what happened and where the money went. You can pretty much forget about getting your money back.

How to Avoid Internet Fraud

If you are online and come across an investment opportunity that looks interesting, here is a list of things to do and consider before pursuing the opportunity further:

1. Don't assume the company online is who they say they are. Check the EDGAR database to find out if the company is registered with the SEC.

2. Do not believe everything you read online or anywhere else. Take time to investigate before you invest.

3. Check with your state securities regulator or the SEC to see if any complaints have been filed against the company, its officers, or promoters.

4. Find out if the person or company offering the investment is licensed to operate in your state.

5. Check your local library for resources that provide information about the company's history. Specifically, you'll want to check

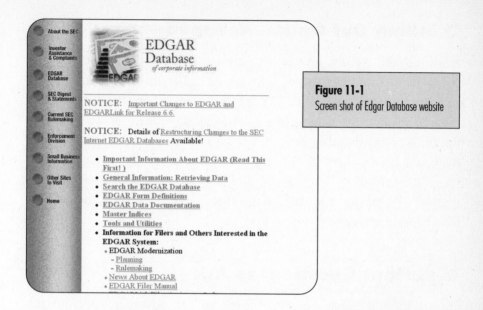

Figure 11-1
Screen shot of Edgar Database website

out their payment history, lawsuits, liens, or judgments. Your local librarian is an excellent source of assistance for locating this type of information.

Time Saver

To check out the EDGAR database of company research and registration information, go to *www.sec.gov* and click on Search EDGAR Archives

6. When you're online, download the information on the investment and print a hard copy. Indicate the date and time you found this data online and keep this for your records. Make sure you get the Internet address or URL in case you need it later.

7. Before you invest make sure you've received a written copy of the prospectus, or the offering circular, and financial statement on the company. If no information is available, just pass altogether.

8. Remember that anyone can set up a Web site and advertise virtually anything they want online. Quite often, no one has bothered to check out the validity or truth about what is being offered.

9. Check with your lawyer, financial advisor, or broker about any investment that you're uncertain about *before* you invest in it.

Checking Out Online Newspapers

In surfing the Net for investment information and advice, you will find hundreds of resources and newsletters that offer investment advice and give stock recommendations. It is important to understand that most of these newsletters are paid to tout a particular investment or stock. This is not often revealed and represents a considerable conflict of interest since the newsletter business receives a great deal of its revenue from its advertisers. It's hard to be completely biased about an investment or company when they're paying your bills. Keep this in mind when you are reading newsletter recommendations.

Important Questions to Ask

Has the online promoter been paid to advertise and tout the investment opportunity, and if so, how much?

Has the online promoter investigated the firm who is offering the investment opportunity? If so, what is their screening process?

What state is the firm offering the investment incorporated in? Once you have that information, you can contact that state's Secretary of State office and find out if the company is incorporated with them and has a current annual report on file.

Here are some other helpful guidelines to use when it comes to online newsletters:

DISCLOSURE OF PAYMENT FOR ADVERTISING

Go To

For a complete list of address and phone numbers of state and federal securities regulators, go to the reference section in the back of this book.

Find out if the newsletter is being paid to tout certain investments. Do they openly disclose any payment they receive, as well as the amount and by whom it was paid? You can pretty much separate the legitimate online newsletters from the others by what they are willing to reveal up front. Disclosure statements are usually indicated somewhere on the Web site itself and are often included in the articles written in the newsletter.

INVESTIGATION OF A COMPANY OR INVESTMENT

Inquire about whether the online newsletter makes a point of checking out the companies and investments it advertises and recommends. Also, what, if any, criteria does it use to base its recommendations on? Regardless of whether it does its own research, it is still best that you perform an independent investigation on a company before you write them a check.

CHECK OUT ONLINE NEWSLETTERS

Occasionally the SEC will find the business tactics of an online newsletter or stock promoter to be less than ethical and will sue them. This information is available through the Enforcement Division of the SEC's homepage. This is a valuable resource that I highly recommend you become familiar with. You can also refer to the SEC's non-EDGAR database for additional information.

Time Saver

To look up information regarding online newsletters that have been sued by the SEC, refer to their Web site at www.sec.gov/con-sumer/jtoptips.htm.

Avoid Recommendations on Thinly Traded Stocks

Thinly traded stocks are by nature more risky than larger, better known company stocks. You should always check with your state securities regulator and conduct your own investigation on these types of stock issues. You can also find a wide variety of independent commercial companies that provide information services to assist you in your research.

Go To

The reference section in the back of this book provides a list of commercial research companies that are available and offer a wide variety of information.

Contact Your State Regulators

Every state has a regulatory office that you can contact to find out if a promoter of a stock or online newsletter has a history of disciplinary actions that you should be aware of. You can check out the disciplinary history of a company through the Central Registration Depository (CRD) at your state regulatory office.

Latest Investment Scams

Time Saver

You can also receive partial disciplinary histories by contacting the National Association of Securities Dealers' (NASD) toll-free public disclosure hotline at 800-289-9999 or contact their Web site at wwwnasdr.com

According to the Federal Trade Commission, more than a billion dollars per year is lost by American investors due to fraudulent investment scams. With the rise of Internet fraud that figure will, no doubt, continue to rise. The Internet has made it easy for fraudsters with their Web sites to entice unsuspecting investors. Many of these fly-by-night operations have Web sites that contain professional quality graphics, audio, and video features to help the investor become easily enticed. Between message boards, chat rooms, and e-mail, you could easily become the recipient of an online investment scam opportunity on any given day of the week.

Many of these online fraudsters operate under more than one company name or use aliases. They create one investment scam for a short period of time, take investors' money, spend it, and close their operation so quickly that they are difficult to detect or track down. Within a short period of time they will bring another scam online, under another name, and the cycle continues. Here are some of the most common investment scams to be on the lookout for.

"Approved" Investment Opportunities

Beware of any investment opportunity that claims to be approved by the SEC or IRS. Neither the SEC nor the IRS approves any investment, ever. These scams have recently been related to the sale of IRA "approved" investments.

Investment Matchmakers

Online matchmaker services are on the rise. These Web sites offer to assist you in finding the perfect investment. Be careful of these types of operations. They often require too much information from you (personal and financial data) and do not disclose enough about their operations, fees, and potential conflicts of interest.

Offshore Investments

These investments can be found everywhere on the Internet. They generally claim to be tax-free, risk-free, and confidential.

Pump and Dump Scams

These are a group of scamsters that peddle small, thinly traded stocks. Generally, these con artists claim to have inside information, get investors to buy thinly traded stocks on the basis of sheer hype, and then watch as they manipulate the stock price up and then sell it quickly (i.e. pump it up and dump it). This usually causes the stock to fall in price, leaving the investors who bought it with a worthless stock.

Prime Bank Notes

These investment scams have become very prevalent. They can be offered in the form of arbitrage contracts, bank debentures, and other types of international currency trading contracts. The people selling these fraudulent investments are often very sophisticated and claim to be involved in international investment banking. They often tell potential investors that these investments are "guaranteed, without risk, and produce large profits." In case you're wondering, however, according to the Federal Reserve, prime bank notes are not real. "The Federal Reserve and other regulators know of no legitimate use of any prime bank related financial instrument," stated Herbert Biern, Deputy Associate Director of the Division of Banking Supervision and Regulation, in an article on investment fraud published on the National Consumer's League Web site.

> **Just a Minute**
>
> If you go online and conduct a search on dogpile.com for "investment opportunities," you will receive hundreds of search results from all the search engines available. I found some of the most amazing investment opportunities by conducting this search. You might consider doing this just as an example of how many offshore investments there are out there. Although some of these investments could be legitimate, they are, nonetheless, an unnecessary risk.

Other possible areas of concern include:

- Viatical settlement scams
- Entertainment fraud
- Ponzi schemes
- Pyramid schemes
- Illegal franchise offerings
- Get rich quick seminars
- Affinity group fraud

If you see online investment advertisements in any of these areas or are approached by a person selling an investment that falls into one of these categories, be careful. Do not give out any personal information or make any decisions to buy without conducting a thorough investigation. Listen to your instincts. If it sounds too good to be true, it usually is.

PART FOUR

KEYS

TO

SUCCESSFUL

TRADING

CHAPTER TWELVE

Trading Investments Online

Pennies don't fall from heaven. They have to be earned on earth.
—Margaret Thatcher, 1979

In this chapter you will begin to place online trades. You'll be guided through the entire trading process from start to finish. You can choose to go through an online trading demo with Ameritrade or proceed to the actual trading screen and place your online trades if you're ready. By the end of this chapter you should be able to successfully execute any order to buy or sell a security.

The Markets and How They Work

The stock market consists of stock exchanges through which the trading of all securities takes place. Each of the U.S. exchanges has specific requirements that companies must meet in order to be listed on that exchange or market.

THE NEW YORK STOCK EXCHANGE (NYSE)

The NYSE is the oldest of the stock exchanges and is located on Wall Street in New York City. It is the heart of all stock market activity. In order to be listed on the NYSE a company must have a minimum of 1.1 million shares publicly held, 2,000 shareholders of 100 shares, and $40 million in market capitalization. There are currently over 3,000 companies listed on the NYSE, most of which consists of the oldest, largest, and most well known companies in the United States.

FYI

It is possible for a company to be listed on more than one exchange. For example, you might find a stock listed on the NYSE also listed on one of the smaller regional exchanges such as the Pacific Exchange located in Los Angeles. Typically, companies are listed on the regional exchanges where they are located and conduct business.

AMERICAN STOCK EXCHANGE (AMEX)

The American Stock Exchange is the rival market of the New York Stock Exchange. The requirements for being listed on AMEX are considerably less stringent, allowing for smaller, lesser known companies to be listed if they meet the minimum requirements of 500,000 publicly held shares and $3 million in market capitalization.

REGIONAL EXCHANGES

Many companies prefer to be listed on the smaller regional exchanges because transactions can often be handled faster and more cost effectively. However, all trades from the regional exchanges are compiled daily into one statistic and listed under the NYSE Composite Trading Table in newspapers such as the *Wall Street Journal*.

The smaller regional exchanges include:

- Midwest Stock Exchange
- Boston Stock Exchange
- Cincinnati Stock Exchange
- Pacific Stock Exchange
- Philadelphia Stock Exchange

NASDAQ—THE ELECTRONIC STOCK EXCHANGE

Unlike the listed exchanges, the NASDAQ does not have a physical location and trading is not conducted through an auction system. The NASDAQ stock market does not have an auction or exchange floor but operates completely through an electronic order taking system. This exchange is operated by the National Association of Securities Dealers (NASD). In 1998, the NASDAQ and AMEX merged, making the NASDAQ the largest of all the exchanges with over 15,000 companies listed. More shares are traded daily on NASDAQ than any other exchange in the United States. A company must have at least 500,000 publicly held shares and a market capitalization of $3 million to be listed on the NASDAQ market. The NASDAQ small-cap minimums makes it much easier for smaller companies to be listed with a minimum requirement of $1 million in market capitalization and 100,000 publicly traded shares.

THE OVER-THE-COUNTER MARKET (OTC)

Many smaller companies are listed on one of the traditional exchanges or the NASDAQ. Nearly 10,000 companies trade in a market referred to as the "over-the-counter" market. These stocks were originally only available for purchase over the counter at a local broker's office. Today these stocks are sold via computer and telephone. OTC stocks are generally cheap stocks that are not highly traded, which makes their pricing harder to come by. Quotes for OTC stocks can be found in the Pink Sheets (published by the National Quotation Bureau) or in the OTC Bulletin Board. Practically all bonds are traded in the OTC market, as are most mutual funds.

FYI

Historically, the NASDAQ attracted mostly new, small companies that were not well known. Today, however, many high profile companies such as Intel, Microsoft, and Cisco are listed on the NASDAQ even though their financial clout easily qualifies them for listing on any major exchange. NASDAQ is no longer just a place to trade stocks, but is where many of the most actively traded stocks are traded daily.

Helpful Hint

Both the Pink Sheets and the OTC Bulletin Board offer real-time online services with real-time quotes for OTC stocks. The Bulletin Board only quotes stocks that are registered with the SEC.

FYI

Once you have selected the investments you desire to buy you only need the correct symbol in order to place the trade. It is not necessary to know what exchange a stock is traded on. When you enter your order online, provided the symbol is correct, it will automatically be routed to the correct exchange.

The stock market and all the exchanges begin each day at 9:30 A.M. and close at 4:00 P.M. (EST). However, it will probably not be long before the U.S. stock market begins to offer around-the-clock trading opportunities. Currently only NASDAQ offers after-hours trading from 4 P.M. to 6:30 P.M. (EST).

Types of Stock Orders

MARKET ORDER

A market order is an order that is placed at the current price of a stock. If you have access to real-time quotes, the price you get from a market order should be the same or close to the quote you received just prior to placing the trade. Variance in price can occur on actively traded stocks or in volatile markets. In any case, a market order must be filled at the best available price.

LIMIT ORDER TO BUY

A limit order establishes how much you are willing to pay for a stock. If you feel a stock's price is likely to change, you can set a limit to the price you are willing to buy it for. Your order will be filled only when the stock reaches that price or lower.

Helpful Hint

An easy way to remember where stocks are traded is that, in general, stock symbols with three or less letters are traded on the NYSE or regional exchange. Stocks with symbols that consist of four letters are traded on the NASDAQ or OTC.

Savvy Investor Tip

If you are placing a limit order to sell, remember to place the order for a price that is higher than the current market quote. Otherwise, what's the point?

LIMIT ORDER TO SELL

A limit order to sell establishes how much you are willing to sell a stock for. Your order will be placed only when the stock reaches that price or higher.

Buy Stop Order

If you want to place a trade above the current market price but within a specific target price, a buy stop order will be triggered at or above a stop price.

Sell Stop Order

A sell stop order is an order that you want to execute below the current market price. A sell stop order is triggered at or below the stop price.

All or None Order (AON)

An all or none order requests that the trade be executed in its entirety or not at all. This type of order is generally used for trades consisting of more than one round lot of stock or more than fifty bonds.

Fill or Kill Order (FOK)

This type of order is used primarily for very large orders in which the investor requests the stock order be filled immediately or not at all.

Immediate or Cancel (IOC)

This type of order is entered when you want as much of the order filled as possible at a requested price. In this case, you have to be willing to accept a partial order of the security you are purchasing.

Helpful Hint

Stop orders are generally placed to protect a profit or to limit a possible loss on a particular stock position. These orders must also indicate whether they must be filled on the day they are placed (called a day order) or held until the order can be filled or you cancel it (called a good till cancelled order or GTC).

FYI

On sell orders you must always enter whether the shares you are selling are held long or short in your account. In other words, is the security owned by you (long) or borrowed (short)?

Placing an Order Online

Right now you can choose to either go online and place your first stock trade (if you already have an account established with Ameritrade or another online broker) or follow along by using the trading demo for practice. To do this, go online now and sign on to Ameritrade at *www.ameritrade.com*. Once you are on Ameritrade's Web site, click on the "trading demo" icon or the "access an account" icon to proceed.

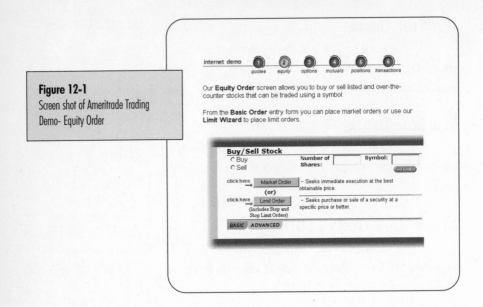

Figure 12-1
Screen shot of Ameritrade Trading Demo- Equity Order

If you want to place an actual trade, click on the "Invest Now" button. To place a stock trade, click on the "Equity Order" button. You will then need to choose one of three order entry options: beginner, intermediate, or advanced. (You can review each of these options, but "beginner" would be most appropriate if you're new at this.)

To enter a buy order to purchase a stock you would enter the following information in the "Buy" order screen:

Helpful Hint

If you want to enter anything other than a market or limit order, you must click on the intermediate or advanced icon. These orders would include all those mentioned in the earlier section of this chapter. If you have any doubts about your ability to do this correctly, contact customer service for assistance.

1. The stock symbol (click on the magnifying glass icon for help finding the right symbol or the Symbol Lookup icon).
2. The number of shares you intend to purchase.
3. The action you are taking: buy or sell.
4. The type of order you desire (i.e., market order, limit). Ameritrade has a great tool to assist you with limit orders called the "limit wizard." Click on the limit wizard's magic wand and try your hand at placing a limit order. (Do not enter this unless you really want to place a limit order.)

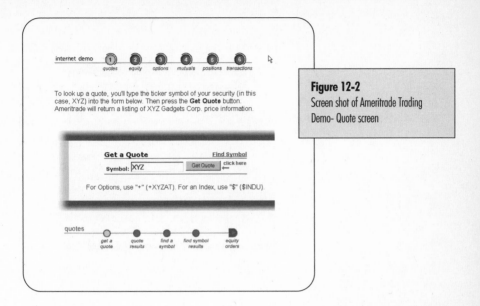

Figure 12-2
Screen shot of Ameritrade Trading
Demo- Quote screen

ORDER ENTRY

Enter the required information into the order screen. However, before you send the actual order make sure you've checked the price of the stock through real-time quotes. Is the current price acceptable to you? If not, you might want to place a limit order. Remember, once you send the order, you own it.

Click on the "Quotes" icon now. Some important facts that the quote screen provides are the current bid and ask price, the last price (most recent), the opening price, the high for the day, the low for the day, the close of the previous day, and the percent change between the current price and the high for the day. The quote screen provides you with additional information as well, which you should take the time to understand as part of your necessary research.

FYI

If you want to check several stock prices, the quote screen at the Ameritrade site will allow you to enter a quote list. You can enter up to thirty-five company symbols. This is a lot easier and faster than doing them one at a time.

VERIFY YOUR TRADES

If you are actually placing a trade now, verify your account number and the order by clicking on "Preview Order." Is everything correct? If so, click on the "Place Order" icon and your order will be processed. Your order will

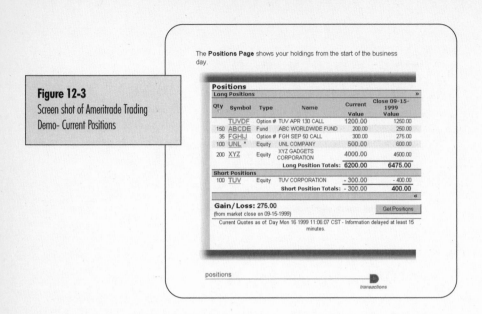

Figure 12-3
Screen shot of Ameritrade Trading
Demo- Current Positions

The **Positions Page** shows your holdings from the start of the business day.

Positions

Long Positions

Qty	Symbol	Type	Name	Current Value	Close 09-15-1999 Value
	TUVDF	Option #	TUV APR 130 CALL	1200.00	1250.00
150	ABCDE	Fund	ABC WORLDWIDE FUND	200.00	250.00
35	FGHIJ	Option #	FGH SEP 50 CALL	300.00	275.00
100	UNL *	Equity	UNL COMPANY	500.00	600.00
200	XYZ	Equity	XYZ GADGETS CORPORATION	4000.00	4500.00
			Long Position Totals:	**6200.00**	**6475.00**

Short Positions

Qty	Symbol	Type	Name	Current Value	Close 09-15-1999 Value
100	TUV	Equity	TUV CORPORATION	- 300.00	- 400.00
			Short Position Totals:	**- 300.00**	**400.00**

Gain/Loss: 275.00
(from market close on 09-15-1999)

Get Positions

Current Quotes as of: Day Mon 16 1999 11:06:07 CST - Information delayed at least 15 minutes.

positions ——————————————————▶

transactions

automatically be cancelled if you do not place your trade within ninety seconds. To check the status of your order, click on the "Order Status" icon. Your confirmation will be e-mailed to you shortly after the trade is filled.

Congratulations! You are now the proud owner of a stock you have traded online by yourself. Make sure you verify that your order was processed correctly by reviewing your confirmation. Also, always print a copy of your order confirmation for your records.

To review your account positions, click on the "Positions" icon now. This screen will provide you with an up-to-date accounting of all of the positions in your account. Once the trade you just made is filled, it will also be reflected on this screen. The position screen will provide you with the following data for each security you own:

- Quantity
- Symbol and name of the security
- Whether the position is long or short
- Current price
- Current value
- Total number of positions you own
- Total value of your account
- Gain or loss in your account as of the market opening

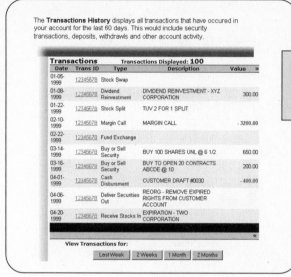

The **Transactions History** displays all transactions that have occured in your account for the last 60 days. This would include security transactions, deposits, withdrawls and other account activity.

Figure 12-4
Screen shot of Ameritrade Trading Demo- Transactions History

To review your trades click on the "transaction" icon. The transaction history will help refresh your memory of what each trade you have placed consisted of. It will give you the following information for each purchase or sale you have made:

- The date you placed the trade
- Whether it was a buy or sell order
- What you bought or sold and at what price it was executed
- What it cost you (or its value)
- Any dividends received
- Any securities received or delivered
- Any cash disbursements
- Any credits and/or debits

Helpful Hint

Your transaction history should be checked for accuracy, as should your monthly statements from your online broker. Mistakes do happen, but chances are unless you catch them, they will go unnoticed.

Pink Sheet Stocks

When placing an order for stocks that are traded on the Pink Sheets or are thinly traded, be aware that it may be difficult to get accurate pricing. If you can't get a quote from your online broker, you can register to use

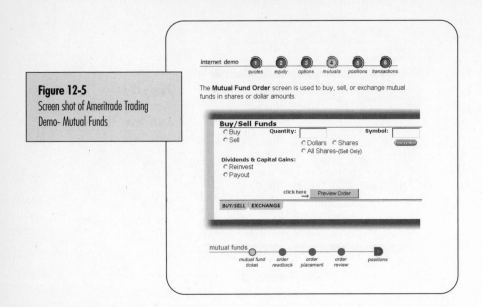

Figure 12-5
Screen shot of Ameritrade Trading
Demo- Mutual Funds

Mutual Fund
orders will not
give you a price
confirmation until
after the market
close at 4:00 P.M.
(EST).

the service provided by the National Quotation
Bureau at *www.otcquote.com/*. Remember that this
type of stock is considered highly speculative.

Placing a Mutual Fund Order

Placing a mutual fund order is very similar to a
stock order. This is the information you will need
to complete the order:

1. The symbol of the mutual fund.
2. The number of shares you wish to buy. You cannot buy in dollar
    amounts online.
3. Whether you want your dividends and capital gains in cash or
    reinvested.
4. The share class (A, B, or C classes are the most common.)

Once you have entered this information on the order entry screen,
click on "Preview Order" to make certain the information is accurate and
you are buying the right mutual fund.

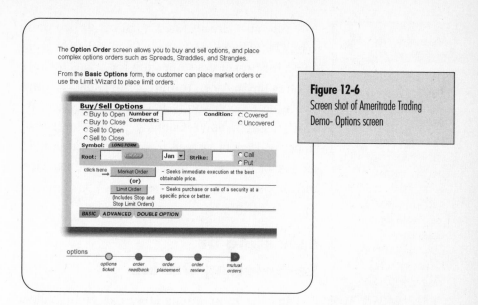

Figure 12-6
Screen shot of Ameritrade Trading Demo- Options screen

Trading Options Online

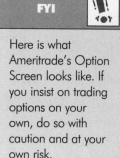

Option trading is a very speculative investment strategy that requires a significant amount of education and/or professional assistance. Most online brokers will allow option trading (if they approve your application), but this author strongly recommends that you pay the $18 and get assistance from an Ameritrade broker by phone. Options trading is a subject and language in and of itself.

Placing a Bond Order

Trading bonds is also an area that requires the assistance of an expert. Most online brokers do not offer the capacity to trade bonds online without the assistance of a broker. Ameritrade offers bond trading through their telephone broker service for a minimum cost of $40, depending on the type of bond and the amount you wish to purchase. Your transactions will show up on your online account and transaction history.

Savvy Investor Tip

Discount online brokers are probably not the best place to trade bonds unless you are a fairly knowledgeable bond investor. Bonds are a specialized investment that requires a lot of research. A good bond broker has access to bond inventory that you may not be able to find on your own.

You must already know what bonds you want to buy before you can trade with an online broker. An online broker does not shop for bonds for you or offer any advice. You are completely on your own even though you're paying for a service. In which case, if you're already paying for assistance, you might as well trade bonds with a full-service broker that can actually provide advice and shop for you, too.

Canceling or Re-Entering Orders

Perhaps the most intimidating aspect of online trading is the potential of making a costly error. That is why it is critical that you *always* preview your order before placing the trade. In the event that you do make an error and place the trade, it is possible to cancel it and re-enter the order. (The exception to this is with market orders that usually fill immediately.) You should be aware, however, that if any order you make fills *before* you have cancelled it, you own it and are responsible for paying for it, so be careful. The best advice in regard to any order entry problem is to contact the customer service line of your online broker for immediate assistance.

Confirmation of Orders

Most online brokers will e-mail you within minutes of placing an order to confirm your trade. You will also receive written confirmation in the mail. Keep all confirmation statements and e-mail you receive. This will save you time and money. Most online companies charge you for duplicate copies.

As you can see, online trading is really quite simple. Even so, it can also be a bit scary. The most important thing to remember when you're trading online is to give yourself plenty of time to place your trades and don't panic if you make a mistake. Help is only a phone call away. Move slowly and stay calm and before long online trading will be second nature.

CHAPTER THIRTEEN

The Wide World of Mutual Funds

I have seen the future; and it works.
—LINCOLN STEFFENS, 1938

In this chapter you will become familiar with the wide spectrum of mutual funds available to online investors. You will learn about the different types of funds, their investment objectives, and how to research and trade them online. By the end of this chapter you will be able to choose the perfect mutual fund for your investment needs and investor profile.

In recent years, mutual funds have become by far the most popular investment vehicle in the United States, with over 73 million shareholders invested. Today there are nearly 8,000 mutual funds to choose from. According to the Investment Company Institute, an organization that addresses the needs and concerns of investment companies and their shareholders, over $6 trillion are invested in mutual funds as of July, 1999. If this year is any indication, with an increase in assets of over 200 billion pouring into stock funds alone (as of June, 1999), it does not appear the popularity of this investment will subside anytime soon.

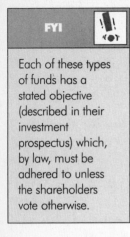

FYI

Each of these types of funds has a stated objective (described in their investment prospectus) which, by law, must be adhered to unless the shareholders vote otherwise.

By definition, a mutual fund is a pool of diversified investments, with a stated objective, that is professionally managed by an investment company. There are many types of mutual funds. The following represents the primary categories:

- growth
- growth & income
- aggressive growth
- balanced
- international
- specialty
- sector

Mutual Fund Advantages

One of the main advantages afforded mutual fund investors is that every shareholder, regardless of how much they have invested in a fund, is treated equally. A shareholder that invests $1,000 into a mutual fund receives the same treatment as a shareholder with $1 million in the same fund. Since all the money is pooled and invested and managed in the same manner, mutual funds are probably the most level playing field offered in the investment world today.

Mutual funds fall into two categories: open-end and closed-end funds. The vast majority of funds are open-ended, which allows investors to buy and sell shares of the fund on any market day. The shares are bought at the current offering price (POP) and sold at the net asset value (NAV). In open-ended mutual funds, both the offering price (the purchase price of the fund) and the NAV (the selling price) are factors that vary daily in accordance with the market.

In closed-end funds, a fixed number of shares are issued and traded on the stock exchange more like a stock. Unlike open-ended funds, the current price of closed-end funds is not the NAV (net asset value), but rather is priced according to supply and demand of its fixed number of shares. Conversely, an open-ended fund has no limit to the number of shares it can issue and is offered on a continuous basis.

Due to the vast number of mutual fund products to choose from, it can be overwhelming for the consumer to know how to select a mutual fund. Unfortunately, far too many people attempt to choose a fund based upon information received in a mutual fund advertisement touting its most recent performance. This can be a big mistake. Chasing a mutual fund's performance and hoping it will repeat itself is not a good method of selection. Many investment magazines provide an annual review of what they consider the top mutual fund performers. Unfortunately, these magazines seldom give more than a one-, three-, and five-year performance history to base their picks on.

> **Helpful Hint**
>
> It is advisable that you avoid choosing a mutual fund purely on short-term rate comparisons. Remember, the last few years have been an exception and is not an accurate measure of long-term historical returns.

Have Realistic Expectations

Investors who believe they can buy a mutual fund that did 35 percent last year and expect that performance to be a precedent will most likely be disappointed. It is more valuable and more realistic to look at the long-term performance of a mutual fund (preferably ten years or more) and see which funds have the best ten-, fifteen-, and twenty-year returns. Why? Because these investments are seasoned and have been through both good and bad markets. They have weathered a few significant market corrections and not only survived but offer a track record that shows whether or not they performed better than average *after* the fact. You do not receive the benefit of this information if you only look at the short-term results. In fact, it is impossible to really know how good the manager of a fund is until a correction or bear market occurs. It is fairly easy to chalk up great returns when the market is hot. The real test is how well they perform when the going gets tough. Quite often, this year's hottest funds move to next year's list of dogs.

The following criteria can be helpful in narrowing the scope and helping you choose mutual funds that fit your investor profile. Keep in mind, mutual funds are not intended to be bought and sold like an individual stock. Although there is no rule about how frequently you can trade mutual funds, to trade them like stock defeats the purpose and is not recommended.

How to Select a Mutual Fund

It is important that you select a mutual fund that fits your investor profile. Given your investor profile, investment objectives and time frame for investing, which type of mutual fund is right for you? Here are the basic mutual funds by type and objective.

Smart Investor Tip

If you have done your homework and selected a well-managed, high-quality fund, price fluctuations should not overly concern you. If you're objective is income, you should be able to rely on a steady check, which is why you buy a bond fund.

BOND FUNDS

Bond Funds are mutual funds that invest primarily in government or corporate bonds (debt instruments) with the objective of providing consistent income to their shareholders in a diversified portfolio. They pay dividends (usually on a monthly basis) and are most suited for investors with an income objective.

A common mistake that investors make is to assume that bond funds are safer than stock funds. This is not necessarily true. Bond funds vary as to their credit worthiness and interest rate risk as well. Both of these risks can effect the price (NAV) of a bond fund or cause the principal to drop.

TAX-FREE MUNICIPAL BOND FUNDS

Tax-free bond funds do the same thing as regular bond funds, but they invest in municipal bonds for the purpose of providing a tax-free income flow to their shareholders. The income received on muni-funds is free from federal tax but may be taxed at the state and local level. Most state muni-bond funds are completely tax free (unless they pay a capital gain, but dividend income is tax-free).

GROWTH FUNDS

Growth funds invest primarily in growth-oriented common stocks for the purpose of long-term capital growth versus income. Most growth stocks pay little or no dividend. These funds attempt to manage assets for the highest rate of return. At the same time, they try to minimize the risk by being diversified and disciplined in their strategy. Most growth funds distribute capital gains, which are taxable to the shareholder.

GROWTH AND INCOME FUNDS

Funds with the objective of providing growth and income invest in high yielding stocks and bonds in order to provide both current income as well as long-term growth. In this case, the stocks and bonds in the portfolio are dividend producing. This type of fund is suitable for any investor but works particularly well for the income investor.

Smart Investor Tip

If you are in a high tax bracket and concerned about the tax impact of capital gains from mutual funds, consider investigating in "tax-managed" growth funds. Some of these funds provide great growth with the intention of never distributing a capital gain. Growth without tax consequences adds up to more money for you and less for Uncle Sam.

BALANCED FUNDS

Balanced funds are invested in both stocks and bonds for the purpose of total diversification. The objective of the bond investments is to balance the fund so that the overall risk is limited without sacrificing the potential for long-term growth. Due to this defensive positioning, balanced funds are not usually on the list of top performers. They do, however, tend to weather a down market better than more aggressive funds.

SPECIALTY FUNDS

Specialty funds are invested in a particular industry or type of security. They can be invested in stock sectors, precious metals, oil and gas, real estate, or any investment sector. These funds can be more volatile or speculative, depending on whether a particular sector is in or out of favor with the economy. This investment is most suited for more aggressive growth investors.

INDEX FUNDS

Index funds are mutual funds that basically invest in the stocks of a particular index such as the S&P 500 or the 30 Dow Industrial stocks. Rather than attempt to beat the market by making their own stock picks, these fund managers invest in the leaders of a particular index. While this is a pretty good strategy overall, it is interesting to note that quite often the growth of an index such as the S&P 500 is driven by only a handful of the stocks in the index.

INTERNATIONAL FUNDS

International funds invest in stocks and bonds of foreign companies and governments, depending on the fund. Some are multi-country funds, others specialize in a particular country or geographic region. International funds that are managed by some of the top fund managers have had great success with their long-term strategy. Due to the ever changing world economy, international funds can be more volatile than domestic funds, but the best of this group usually performs very well for the disciplined long-term investor.

Savvy Investor Tip

You can get a Morningstar report online at www.morningstar.com, or from your financial advisor or online brokerage company if they provide them. In addition to ratings, Morningstar provides comprehensive data on the fund's manager(s), their tenure, the major investment holdings in the fund's portfolio, how the assets are allocated, and their historical returns.

Important Facts to Consider

GET A MORNINGSTAR REPORT

Get a Morningstar report on any mutual fund that you are considering. Morningstar is an independent rating service that provides ratings on most mutual funds. Their ratings range from five stars for the highest to one star for the lowest rating. All things considered, why invest in a mutual fund that doesn't have at least a four or five star rating? This will help you eliminate a lot of funds that just don't make the grade.

CHECK OUT THE MANAGEMENT OF THE FUND

Is the fund managed by a team or a single fund manager? How long has the team been managing it? If it's an individual, how long has the person

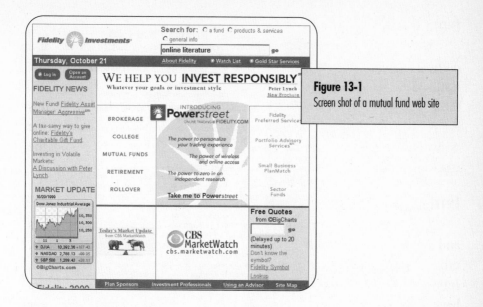

Figure 13-1
Screen shot of a mutual fund web site

been the manager? What is his or her history of managing assets? One thing to consider is that many fund managers today have less than five years experience managing large amounts of money. Many are in their early thirties (or younger) and were still in high school during the last significant market correction. It is yet to be seen how these inexperienced mangers will fare in the next big market correction. However, in all fairness to these young managers, they generally come from the best schools, have excellent credentials, and are some of the country's brightest minds. The question is, who are you most comfortable with managing your money? Research the funds you're interested in and decide what fits your comfort level. You can find some of this information in a Morningstar report, in the fund's annual report, or at the investment company's Web site.

READ THE PROSPECTUS

Although reading a mutual fund prospectus is about as enticing as a trip to the dentist, it too is required to maintain a healthy portfolio. It is important that you understand the objective of a fund before you invest in it. It is essential that you understand and agree with its investment strategy. Read the fine print. Some funds have the ability to invest more speculatively than you might imagine. If you don't read the prospectus, you won't know what the parameters are.

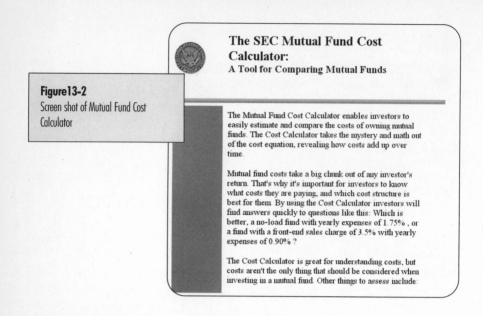

The SEC Mutual Fund Cost Calculator:
A Tool for Comparing Mutual Funds

Figure 13-2
Screen shot of Mutual Fund Cost Calculator

The Mutual Fund Cost Calculator enables investors to easily estimate and compare the costs of owning mutual funds. The Cost Calculator takes the mystery and math out of the cost equation, revealing how costs add up over time.

Mutual fund costs take a big chunk out of any investor's return. That's why it's important for investors to know what costs they are paying, and which cost structure is best for them. By using the Cost Calculator investors will find answers quickly to questions like this: Which is better, a no-load fund with yearly expenses of 1.75% , or a fund with a front-end sales charge of 3.5% with yearly expenses of 0.90% ?

The Cost Calculator is great for understanding costs, but costs aren't the only thing that should be considered when investing in a mutual fund. Other things to assess include:

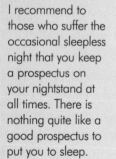

FYI

I recommend to those who suffer the occasional sleepless night that you keep a prospectus on your nightstand at all times. There is nothing quite like a good prospectus to put you to sleep.

LOAD VERSUS NO-LOAD

Contrary to popular belief (to which the media has provided an endless supply of misinformation and hype), there is no such thing as a true "no-load" mutual fund. You can stop looking. The real cost of investing (and there is one, trust me) is in the fine print of the prospectus. Great strides have been taken to fool the public about this subject and this author would like to assist you in developing a true understanding of how to calculate the true cost of investing in any mutual fund. Rather than give you my own version of how to do this, check out the new SEC mutual fund calculator site at *www.sec.gov/mfcc/mfcc-int.htm*

The Mutual Fund Cost Calculator provided on this site is totally objective and a consumer friendly way of determining the true cost of investing. This calculator allows you to assess other important information as well, such as:

- how long it will take to achieve your investment goal;
- the type and asset mix of a given mutual fund;

Mutual fund costs take a big chunk out of any investor's return. That's why it's important for investors to know what costs they are paying, and which cost structure is best for them. By using the Cost Calculator investors will find answers quickly to questions like this: Which is better, a no-load fund with yearly expenses of 1.75% , or a fund with a front-end sales charge of 3.5% with yearly expenses of 0.90% ?

The Cost Calculator is great for understanding costs, but costs aren't the only thing that should be considered when investing in a mutual fund. Other things to assess include:

- the number of years needed to reach an investment goal,
- the type of stocks, bonds, or other securities that the fund buys,
- the risk of the fund,
- the fit between the fund and the investor's portfolio (diversification),
- the fund company or portfolio manager who runs the fund,
- the fund's track record or performance over time, and
- the types of services offered by the fund company.

Figure 13-2
Screen shot of Mutual Fund Cost Calculator

- the relative risk factor;
- if the fund is compatible with your investor profile;
- information on the fund manager;
- the long term track record of the fund;
- how to compare the cost of one fund to another.

CALCULATE YOUR COSTS

Consider taking a highly rated load fund from the American Funds family and compare it to a highly rated no-load fund of your choice. You might be surprised to find that a good load fund often (certainly not always) outperforms and costs less in the long run. Don't rule out load funds simply because you think no-load is best. That is not always true and may cause you to miss out on some of the best fund managers around.

Helpful Hint

This site www.sec.gov/mfcc/mfcc-int.htm offers you completely unbiased facts so you don't fall prey to the often ill-informed opinions of others. This organization is trying to help clear up the cost confusion by providing this valuable resource. They are not in the business of trying to sell you something.

USE HELPFUL ONLINE MUTUAL FUND TOOLS

A great online source for helping narrow your mutual fund search using certain criteria is the INVESTools Web site at *www.investools.com*. This site has a mutual fund program that allows you to conduct a search by:

- Morningstar rating;
- minimum annual return you desire;
- period of time to reach your goal;
- minimum annual yield (for making income fund selections);
- your objective (growth, growth and income, income, etc.).

The program will then provide a list of all funds that meet your criteria, which can be printed out for further research. In addition to this great resource, this site also offers many other helpful tools for online investors.

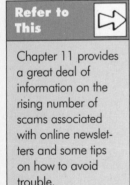

Refer to This

Chapter 11 provides a great deal of information on the rising number of scams associated with online newsletters and some tips on how to avoid trouble.

READ RELIABLE RESEARCH

There are so many mutual fund market timing newsletters that it is impossible to list them all. The good news is you don't need any of them. It is better to avoid newsletters since they are mostly advertisements and not research. The vast majority of publications in this category are paid to tout certain investments. This is not the kind of unbiased research you need to help you make good investment choices. If you insist on using these sources, check them out first and make certain they are legitimate.

Mutual Funds: The Investment for Everyone

Mutual funds have proven to be the best investment product ever introduced to the investing public. They offer affordable, systematic investing that virtually anyone can participate in. Some mutual funds will allow you to invest on a monthly basis for as little as $25 or $50 per month (also referred to as dollar cost averaging.) Regardless of your investor profile, there is a mutual fund out there that should meet your needs. Mutual funds are also a great way to save for your child's education. With the cost of higher education skyrocketing annually, mutual funds are a great way to grow your money. You can invest the money in a custodial account with no limit as to how much you can invest, or set up an educational IRA that allows you to save up to $500 per year tax free.

Some of the other advantages to investing in mutual funds are:

- diversification of assets
- flexibility of investment options
- low investment minimums
- exchange privileges (can move from one fund to another at no cost)
- automatic investment programs
- systematic withdrawal programs
- dollar cost averaging
- automatic reinvestment of dividends and capital gains
- easy to manage custodial accounts
- mutual fund retirement accounts (IRAs, Roth IRAs, SEPs)

Speaking of retirement planning, if you pull up the retirement calculator site located at *www.kiplinger.com,* it will tell you how much money you'll have for retirement if you invest the maximum contribution of $2,000 per year into an IRA. I ran this calculation for myself and quickly determined that an IRA alone will not meet my retirement needs. However, if I invest $10,000 per year for the next twenty years, I'll have over $500,000 by the time I'm sixty. This exercise will help you learn if an IRA alone is enough for retirement. If not, you'll need to find more ways to save and invest so that you too may grow old gracefully or retire to the pursuit of reckless adventure.

Whatever your investment goals and objectives are, mutual funds are excellent investment vehicles for almost any investor at any age or stage of life. Carefully follow the directions outlined in this chapter, its resources and criteria, and you should easily find the best mutual fund for you.

CHAPTER FOURTEEN
IPO's—The Wild Ride

A throw of the dice will never eliminate chance.
　　　　　　　　　　—STEPHANE MALLARME, 1897

In this chapter you will learn how to participate in one of the most coveted investment opportunities available today. While initial public offerings (called IPOs) are certainly not for every investor, they are a hot investment topic. If you decide to pursue IPOs as an investment, this chapter will provide you with the basics of how to participate.

Historically, initial public offerings (IPOs) have been an investment opportunity offered mostly to the favored clients of participating brokerage firms, investment bankers, and venture capitalists. This exclusive club generally picked the cherry IPOs, divied them up amongst themselves and their clients, and left the pits to be picked up by the general public. Fortunately, even some of the pits grew to be fruitful investments. While everyone involved in purchasing IPOs has risk exposure, the playing field has never been a level one. The greatest potential of a typical IPO is buying into the offering before it goes public. Unfortunately, that simply has not been available for most investors.

While IPOs can offer tremendous investment opportunity, they are considerably speculative and should not be included in every investor's portfolio. Just like any other investment, IPOs should be selected only if they suit your investor profile and risk tolerance. It is important to know that while IPOs have created many millionaires, studies indicate that roughly half of all IPOs fail or significantly underperform compared to equity investments with an established track record.

Advantages and Disadvantages of Going Public

The main reason a company decides to go public is to raise capital for expansion and/or for the research and development of new products and services. In exchange for this new capital infusion, a company effectively gives up a significant piece of its ownership. In the process it also forfeits its autonomy and ability to control the company's direction. You should be aware of some of the other disadvantages companies face in going public. These disadvantages include:

Helpful Hint

Go to the SEC's EDGAR database www.sec.gov for a complete list of information provided in public offering filings.

LOSS OF CONFIDENTIALITY

A public company must disclose all of its material facts in order to convince investors that it is worthy of their investment and financial commitment.

INCREASED LEGAL LIABILITY

The participants of an IPO are all jointly and severally liable for each other's actions and may be sued for any misinformation or omissions provided to the public.

INCREASED VISIBILITY

As a public company, the performance of a given company can be easily tracked and monitored by other companies. As a result, it may become the target of an unwanted takeover.

For most companies, the advantages of going public generally outweigh the disadvantages, which is why we have witnessed a significant rise in companies going public. In addition to raising much needed capital, companies also receive the following benefits after they go public:

INCREASE IN PUBLIC AWARENESS

Public companies generally have a much higher public profile than private companies, which may add to their potential for new customers. Additionally, going public can also create a venue for new shareholders as more people learn about and want to own their stock.

CREATE SOURCE OF FUTURE CAPITAL

If a company's first IPO is successful, it is easy for the company to issue more stock in a secondary offering once the stock is more seasoned. Not only is it easier to raise capital the second time around, but most companies are able to raise significantly more capital (often more than three times the original IPO).

EXECUTIVE CASH OUT

It is considerably easier for an officer or key executive to sell his or her shares in a public company. Key executives often desire to sell stock in order to diversify their holdings, change their lifestyle, or retire.

POSSIBLE MERGER OR ACQUISITION

By virtue of being public, a small company hoping to become part of a larger organization may become a candidate for a merger with another firm. Public companies have the ability to scrutinize each other, with larger corporations on the watch for compatible smaller companies that show top performance. Smaller nonpublic companies are generally not visible enough to be observed as a merger possibility.

Savvy Investor Tip

It is not a good sign if too many key executives in an organization are selling their stock. This can be interpreted negatively by the market. For example, insider selling often indicates that something is up with the company or its management that may adversely effect the stock price.

How IPOs Work

Once a company decides to go public it takes three to six months of preparation before a company is ready to proceed with its offering. A company must present its best face to attract investors. Since the underwriters of an IPO are responsible for selling all the shares it commits to, a good deal of effort and planning must be done to ensure the successful sale of the new issue.

Noteworthy Tip

There is a twenty day cooling off period before anything other than the preliminary prospectus can be used to solicit indications of interest in the issue.

After the proper documents have been filed with the SEC, the underwriting firm, along with the syndication group (the team formed to help sell the issue), decides when the issue should be taken public based upon market conditions.

During times of great volatility, it is not uncommon for pending IPOs to be cancelled. The timing of an IPO is critical to its success. Following the 1987 crash, almost all IPOs were cancelled. After all, who wants to test out a new boat after witnessing the sinking of the *Titanic*?

PRICING THE ISSUE

When the timing is deemed suitable, the next step is to determine the pricing of the issue. This is where investors have to be careful. Generally speaking, it is easier for the underwriter to sell lower priced issues. This also makes it easier for brokerages firms to give their allotments (of shares) to their best clients. For example, it would not be uncommon for an IPO to be priced in the $20 dollar range, and the allotments sold at that price, and then on the day the issue goes public for the stock to soar two to three times that price. When a stock goes hot, as this kind of significant rise is referred to, it will often create a buying frenzy that one should approach with caution. It is difficult for investors to remember that during times like this most of these IPOs often have no financially sound reason to shoot up in price so dramatically. It is of utmost importance to remember that these new companies, no matter how good they appear, have no proven track record and may drop significantly in price or fail completely. In any case, pricing for IPOs is a nebulous science at best, and for the average investor it is very difficult to ascertain if you are paying a fair price for an IPO or not.

Guidelines for Buying an IPO

If you really want to invest in an IPO, go back to the basics of research and do your homework first. Read the prospectus. Compare the prospectus of other successful IPOs to one you are considering. Review the section in the prospectus that refers to the amount of stock being sold in the offering by its management (located in "The Offering" section under "Principal and Selling Stockholders"). If the company's prospects were truly great, why would the existing stockholders or management be selling out?

Look closely at the management of the company, their history, and their compensation. Officers of publicly traded companies should be compensated on performance. If they are already making megabucks, how hard do they need to work to make the company successful for their stockholders? This information is also located in the prospectus.

Do your own research on the company. Analyze the fundamentals of the company compared to other stocks in its industry. How large is the company's customer base? Make certain they are not overly dependent on one or two large customers, because if they lose one, there go half the company's sales.

What are they going to do with the capital they are receiving from the IPO? If they don't have a solid plan, don't go there.

What firm is underwriting the deal? Stick with the major brokerage firms like Merrill Lynch or Goldman Sachs. Also look into deals offered by venture capital firms such as Bill Hambrecht's new IPO company, OpenIPO, which now takes companies public online. These people know what they are doing and stand a far better chance of succeeding with a new issue than a small firm with a significantly smaller distribution capability.

FYI

Most online trading sites such as E*trade participate in IPOs as well. If you know you want to trade IPOs online, make sure your online broker has this capability before you open an account.

Figure 14-1
Screen shot of OpenIPO web site

Ask yourself these questions:

- What is the marketing potential for the IPO?
- How does it compare to its competition?
- How do the company's products or services compare to established companies in the same industry?
- What do they have (patents, technology, etc.) that sets them apart?
- Are there any known risks to the IPO based upon the nature of its business either legally, financially, or economically?
- Are there any recent developments about the company or its product that might have an affect on the IPO's performance?
- Check out the recent news.

Lastly, do you believe in the company, its product or service? Are you already or will you become a customer yourself? Invest in things you believe in, buy, or think there is a need for, and chances are you will have a successful IPO along the way.

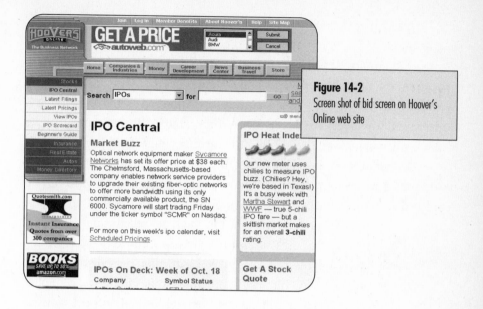

Figure 14-2
Screen shot of bid screen on Hoover's Online web site

Here are some good places to shop for IPO's:

OpenIPO (www.openipo.com). Bill Hambrecht, the founder of the venture capital firm Hambrecht & Quist, has created the first and most interesting IPO site to appear online to date. Hambrecht has taken many companies public in his career. His vision for OpenIPO is to provide a level playing field for all investors to participate in IPOs, regardless of their financial clout.

OpenIPO is an electronic underwriting service that intends to use technology as a means of distributing information to the everyday consumer, as opposed to the process that has previously catered to the few and the wealthy. Conducted as an auction, at OpenIPO anyone can put in a bid to purchase a particular IPO offered on this site. Essentially all bidders are given equal access and the price of the IPO is driven by the demand for the offering. Similar to an auction, the "winners" are those who are willing to place the highest bid. However, this is a silent auction where bids are kept secret and those who win the bid pay the same price, which is the amount of lowest winning bid. Anyone looking to participate in IPOs will find this site to be both easy to use and equitable.

To participate you must open an account with one of their participating brokerages, which are listed on their site, along with a complete listing of upcoming IPOs.

*Hoover's Online (*www.ipocentral.hoovers.com*).* This user-friendly Web site provides quick, up-to-date information on IPOs by industry, underwriter, or location. If you know the name of the company or its symbol, you can look up the information directly online. Each day Hoover's has a commentary on the most recent IPOs that includes a featured IPO, newly priced issues, and IPOs that have started trading. They also have a scorecard section that you can click on and check out the best and worst performing IPOs in the most recent quarter.

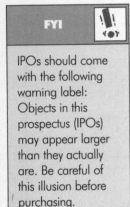

FYI

IPOs should come with the following warning label: Objects in this prospectus (IPOs) may appear larger than they actually are. Be careful of this illusion before purchasing.

*IPO Central (*www.ipocentral.hoovers.com*).* This is a handy Web site that provides the latest SEC filings of companies that intend to go public. Their database offers additional information as well, such as company profiles and current stock quotes.

*Yahoo!Finance (*www.yahoo.finance.com*).* Yahoo!'s finance site provides easy access and information on upcoming IPOs. While you're there, utilize their research tools to further investigate an IPO that has piqued your interest.

Also check out the Web sites of E*Offering *www.eoffering.com* and AlertIPO *www.alertipo.com*.

IPOs are perhaps the most tantalizing and sexy investment around, quick to seduce even the most sophisticated investor. However, the reality is that for every amazon.com love affair, there are ten sad stories of those who got left at the altar empty handed. Think this investment move through carefully before testing.

PART FIVE

STRATEGIES

FOR

MANAGING

YOUR

PORTFOLIO

CHAPTER FIFTEEN

Everyday Trading Strategies

*Thanks to modern technology, history now comes equipped with
a fast-forward button.*

—GORE VIDAL, 1992

In this chapter you will learn trading strategies that will assist you in
managing your investments. You will also be given tips for managing
your emotions during volatile markets. It is essential to develop an
investment philosophy that suits your investor profile. The tips and
strategies provided in this chapter will help you stick to your plan
regardless of market conditions.

Deciding your investment strategy and sticking to it is the key to
successful portfolio management. Many claim to be long-term
investors, yet they tend to watch over and worry about their portfolios
on a daily basis. If you determine that you are indeed a "buy-and-hold"
investor, you would be wise to buy quality investments, perhaps the
most attractive growth stock buys available at the time, and simply hold
those investments indefinitely. Fretting about the market is contrary to
taking a long-term investment approach and will not serve your purpose. As a buy-and-hold investor, you might consider selling a position
in your portfolio under the following conditions:

Helpful Hint

Buy-and-hold
investors should
have a low portfolio
turnover. They
should only sell an
investment when
something signifi-
cant changes in the
fundamentals of the
investment or in their
personal financial
objectives.

- when the fundamentals of a stock strongly indicate that the company may be approaching a significant financial or management change that could adversely effect the stock;
- if a stock you own becomes overvalued by the market, you might consider selling it. That does not mean the stock will not continue to go up. It very well might. However, if a stock is overvalued, it is not fundamentally worth the price it is selling for;
- Your own financial situation changes, requiring you to pursue another investment strategy.

Other Fundamentals to Consider

The key fundamentals that should be taken into consideration in assessing a stock include:

    price
    p/e ratio
    book value
    earnings per share
    return on equity
    profit margin

PRICE

In evaluating the price of a stock it is important to look at how its price compares to other stocks in the same industry. In addition, you should evaluate the stock's price in relationship to its future prospects. Are there significant indications that the company's stock price might be increasing in the near future?

P/E Ratio

The price/earnings ratio describes the relationship between the current stock price and its earnings per share and is easy to calculate. You can determine the p/e ratio by dividing the current price of the stock by its earnings per share figure. A low p/e ratio is generally considered more desirable. However, p/e ratio alone does not determine whether one stock is better priced than another.

Book value

The book value of a stock is one indicator of whether or not a stock is likely to be profitable in the future. Basically, a company's book value is the difference between its assets and liabilities. If a company has a low book value and is burdened by debt, it is unlikely to be profitable until its revenue increases enough to reduce the debt. On the other hand, if the company has a low book value but its assets are underestimated, it may be seen as an attractive buy.

Earnings Per Share

If you divide a stock's net earnings by its number of outstanding shares, you will know its true earnings. A company whose earnings per share increase annually is usually in an attractive growth phase. If the earnings growth is sporadic, you can expect greater price fluctuation.

Return on Equity

To calculate the return on equity of a company simply divide the earnings per share by the book value of the stock (assets minus liabilities.) A company must have a high return on equity in order to be viewed as a good growth stock.

Savvy Investor Tip

A very high p/e ratio is often indicative that a stock is significantly overpriced. It is not uncommon these days to see p/e ratios of Internet stocks well over 100. This may prove to be precarious for investors investing in high p/e stocks. Be cautious.

Helpful Hint

Look carefully at the expenses of a company to help determine how a company spends its capital. Are expenses in line with sales growth?

PROFIT MARGIN

This is the bottom line. Is the company consistently profitable and is its profit margin growing?

Keys to Successful Portfolio Management

The investment management industry has many different schools of thought on the subject of investment strategy. No one approach is successful 100 percent of the time. However, there are some basic tried and true tenets that may lead to a higher rate of success. These are among the best:

1. Buy companies, not stock. If you like a company, its products, and management, you'll be more committed to it.
2. Buy performance. Does the company have a good history of consistent performance?
3. Buy the future. Does the company have better than average long-term prospects for the future?
4. Buy the leaders. Is the stock a leader in its industry or have prospects that could position it as a leader in its industry?
5. Buy management. Is the management of the company experienced and well perceived by its employees and the public?
6. Buy profit margins. Does the company have a consistent and growing profit margin?
7. Buy value. Is the stock a good buy and is it the right time to buy it?

Helpful Hint

Of course, liking a company is not enough. No matter how much you like a stock, its history of performance, current financial condition, and future prospects must support your decision to buy or sell.

Follow these simple guidelines and you will most likely find yourself owning and profiting from some very good companies.

Managing Economic Factors

Once you've been investing for a while you will realize that economic news can wreak havoc with your portfolio. Regardless of how good a company is doing, virtually any stock can get hit by a wave of bad economic news. Certain economic factors tend to affect the market and stock prices more than others:

Consumer price index
Consumer credit
Producer price index
Unemployment rate
Durable goods orders
New factory orders

THE CONSUMER PRICE INDEX (CPI)

The consumer price index is by far the most widely used measure of inflation. In addition, the CPI has the greatest influence on economic policy decisions. The CPI is complied by the Bureau of Labor and Statistics on a monthly basis. These monthly figures reflect economic price trends in consumer goods and services.

CONSUMER CREDIT INDEX

The consumer credit index is seasonally adjusted and indicates the level of consumer credit spending to pay for goods and services (as opposed to cash spending.) An increase in this index tends to be favorable and reflects optimism on the part of consumers. Conversely, when people are not confident in the economy, they tend to spend less.

PRODUCER PRICE INDEX (PPI)

The PPI measures the cost of raw materials. If the cost of materials is on the rise, a subsequent rise in prices can be anticipated. This is also an inflationary sign.

FYI

A rise in the CPI creates concern of inflation. Such news is not well received by the stock market, which often reacts adversely. You would be wise to pay attention to upcoming news from the Federal Reserve regarding inflation. In inflationary times, the Fed is likely to raise interest rates. Typically, this means a "green light" special may be just around the corner, providing bargains on some of your favorite stocks.

FYI

Ironically, the higher the unemployment rate, the better the economy. (This is why I could never be an economist. Celebrating the number of people out of work is incongruous with the thought of popping a bottle of good champagne.) But a rise in the unemployment rate is generally viewed as more favorable for the economy than a drop in unemployment, which sparks fears of inflation.

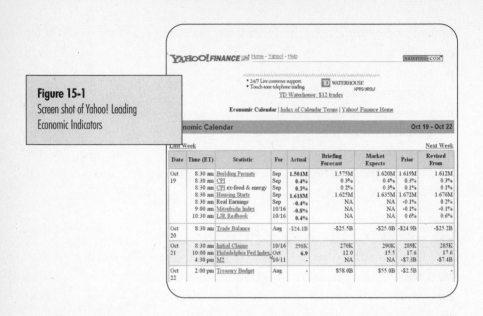

Figure 15-1
Screen shot of Yahoo! Leading
Economic Indicators

Date	Time (ET)	Statistic	For	Actual	Briefing Forecast	Market Expects	Prior	Revised From
Oct 19	8:30 am	Building Permits	Sep	1.501M	1.575M	1.620M	1.619M	1.612M
	8:30 am	CPI	Sep	0.4%	0.3%	0.4%	0.3%	0.3%
	8:30 am	CPI ex-food & energy	Sep	0.3%	0.2%	0.3%	0.1%	0.1%
	8:30 am	Housing Starts	Sep	1.618M	1.625M	1.635M	1.672M	1.676M
	8:30 am	Real Earnings	Sep	-0.4%	NA	NA	-0.1%	0.2%
	9:00 am	Mitsubishi Index	10/16	-0.8%	NA	NA	-0.1%	-0.1%
	10:30 am	LJR Redbook	10/16	0.4%	NA	NA	0.6%	0.6%
Oct 20	8:30 am	Trade Balance	Aug	-$24.1B	-$25.5B	-$25.0B	-$24.9B	-$25.2B
Oct 21	8:30 am	Initial Claims	10/16	298K	270K	290K	289K	285K
	10:00 am	Philadelphia Fed Index	Oct	6.9	12.0	15.5	17.6	17.6
	4:30 pm	M2	10/11	-	NA	NA	-$7.3B	-$7.4B
Oct 22	2:00 pm	Treasury Budget	Aug	-	$58.0B	$55.0B	-$2.5B	-

UNEMPLOYMENT RATE

This statistic indicates the increase or decrease in the number of jobs and how different industries are impacting employment.

Smart Investor Tip

One reason you might want to keep abreast of economic news is this: inflationary news of any kind usually creates a subsequent drop in the market. Although these drops are often temporary, they can create price breaks and good buying opportunities. A drop in the market is a good time to see if your favorite stock is on sale.

DURABLE GOODS ORDERS

This economic indicator measures the number of new orders of a variety of manufactured goods, from transportation to machinery. An increase in orders is viewed as a positive sign of economic expansion.

NEW FACTORY ORDERS

Similar to the durable goods indicator, this index reports the number of new orders for consumer goods and reflects consumer confidence.

Changes and fluctuations in these economic indicators (as well as others not mentioned here) have major implications and affects on the stock market, both good and bad. As an investor, you can follow these economic indicators online as a part of managing your portfolio. Although even professionals cannot easily predict the outcome or direction of the economy, paying attention to these factors can assist you in your overall portfolio strategy and management.

While it is important to be aware of changes in the economy, a good investor will not change his or her overall investment strategy simply due to economic trends. It is important to always consider all other fundamentals of an investment and not overreact to economic news. In the long run, a good portfolio should weather whatever economic storm is on the horizon.

Market Cycle Strategies

Market cycles are virtually impossible to predict and can typically only be explained in hindsight. No one has a crystal ball that will predict the next stock market crash or bear market. What economists and research analysts do have to offer are their beliefs and opinions, some of which are accurate some of the time. In the end, the stock market is driven largely by two factors: fear and greed. Bull markets are fueled largely by greed and bear markets are fueled largely by fear. People buy on optimistic greed and sell on the pessimism created by fear.

While both of these emotions exist in the stock market every single day, when one emotional factor (generally driven by an abundance of good or bad news) begins to be persistent and pervasive, a market cycle shifts in accordance. For example, if fear of inflation and rising interest rates continue to create sustained pressure in the market, after a while, investors lose confidence, become anxious, and begin to sell out of fear. If the selloff becomes prolonged, it can and has created significant market corrections.

Riding the Markets

Historically, there have been far more bull markets than bear markets. A bull market generally takes longer to reach its high than a bear market does to drop to its low. The best advice regarding market cycles is the simplest: ride them out. If you want to

FYI

In truth, most investors who sell in market downturns lose more money than they would have gained by staying put (if they were in quality investments, that is).

FYI

A real bear market generally doesn't kick in until the stock market has at least a 20 percent correction. At this point, with the Dow high reaching 11,000, that would require a drop of over 2,000 points. The market was at 1,738 when the 1987 crash hit creating a 22.6 percent loss in the market.

Helpful Hint

Keep a "watch list" of stocks that you are interested in but are a bit pricey. If you have the patience to wait, you might get to take advantage of a temporary trough and get to buy the stock at a discount.

protect a profit, a stop loss or limit order can provide some protection. These orders can establish a limit as to how far a stock can drop before a sell is triggered or prevent you from buying a stock at too high a price.

When to Buy or Sell

The best investment strategy is one that attempts to buy the best companies, at the best prices. This often means being on the lookout for and taking advantage of temporary weaknesses and price drops. For example, certain technology stocks are notorious for having major price fluctuations brought on by earnings reports that ripple through the tech sector like an earthquake followed by a series of aftershocks. Such fluctuations are generally short term and not represented by any fundamental problem with the underlying stocks. As a result, this often presents some bargain opportunities for investors sitting with money on the sideline.

Trading in Volatile Markets

The stock market has become increasingly volatile with wide fluctuations in prices occurring more frequently than ever before. It is important that you understand the types of problems associated with fast moving markets and what to anticipate. When the markets are volatile and the volume of stocks being purchased and sold is unusually high the following problems can occur:

Delays in pricing
Problems with executions of trades
Confirmation delays
Difficulty accessing your online account

Here are some guidelines for managing your portfolio during volatile markets:

1. Place limit orders. This will prevent you from paying more for a stock than you intended or from selling a stock below a certain price target. Avoid placing market orders in times like this.

2. Online access problems do occur so know what your trading alternatives are with your online broker. Most companies offer telephone trade options and faxed orders or you may need to request the assistance of a broker by phone.

3. If you don't get a confirmation on a trade, do not assume the order did not go through and place another order. If the first trade was placed, you will end up owing for both trades. If you are uncertain about a transaction, contact your online customer service department for assistance before you proceed.

> **Helpful Hint**
>
> Be proactive in the area of margin trading or risk having securities sold at a loss with no recourse. This is another reason you should be very cautious before signing a margin agreement.

4. If you have a margin account, be aware that you may receive a margin call if your portfolio value drops below the minimum maintenance requirement. Your online broker may sell securities in order to cover the margin call. (Remember: they have the legal right to do this.)

Managing Your Emotions

Investing can be a highly emotional experience. Most people underestimate this fact and are often unprepared for their emotional response to market circumstances. It is often difficult to remain calm and rational during a market selloff while watching your portfolio drop and your profits disappear. Here are some tips for managing your emotions on tough market days when you're tempted to sell everything and run for cover:

1. Every market correction eventually recovers. Historically, the average recovery has taken less than eighteen months.

2. If you sell, where will you put your money? A 5 percent CD is not going to get you where you want to be financially. (After taxes and inflation, you may very well have a negative return.)

3. Time and patience are two of the most important disciplines of investing. If you've got the time, cultivate the patience. It will pay off.

4. If you are overly stressed and losing sleep, you need to get professional advice (no, not a therapist, a financial advisor). If you can't trust your own investment strategy, you need guidance. You may find that you are simply investing in a manner that is too risky for your investor profile.

5. Avoid the temptation to invest with the pack. Do what you know and trust to be good for you. Just because your friends are investing in highflying Internet stocks and IPOs doesn't mean it's right for you. Besides, people generally only tell you their success stories. You seldom get the lowdown on the losses.

6. If you find yourself becoming a little too obsessed with your investments and your life is getting out of balance (especially if you're day trading and you have no life), consider taking the following questionnaire to determine if you have a gambling problem.

Investment Gambling Questionnaire

(Answer true or false to each question.)

1. I spend most of my day trading investments and have little or no social life. True/False

2. I am preoccupied with my investments even when I am attempting to do other things. True/False

3. My family and/or friends have expressed concern over my obsession with investing. True/False

4. I feel anxious and irritable if I am forced to be away from trading my investments for any extended time period.

5. I have major mood swings that are related to how well my investments are performing. True/False

6. I am a highly speculative investor. True/False

7. I often risk more money than I can afford to lose. True/False

8. I trade aggressively on margin. True/False

9. I have borrowed from my credit cards to invest. True/False

10. I have had more than one financial crisis resulting from a margin call. True/False

11. I have suffered significant losses and have lied about it to family and friends. True/False

12. I have tried to stop investing compulsively and have been unable to quit. True/False

13. I believe I may have a gambling problem. True/False

Six or more true answers indicate you may have a gambling problem.

To seek help contact a therapist in your community or Gambler's Anonymous listed in your local telephone directory.

If you answer true to more than three of these questions, you should be cautious and aware that you may be headed toward a gambling problem. Stop while you're ahead and still can.

As you progress in your knowledge and skill as an investor, you may want to pursue more

Refer To

To locate additional and more sophisticated investment strategy resources, both online and off, go to the reference section in the back of this book.

sophisticated investment strategies that have not been covered in this chapter. The more technical investment strategies should be studied in depth before you attempt to implement them. However, when you are ready, you will find an abundance of information available on the Internet to assist you with your continuing investment education. Good luck in your online adventure. May all your trades be profitable.

CHAPTER SIXTEEN

Troubleshooting and Problem Solving

Put all your eggs in the one basket, and WATCH THAT BASKET.

—Mark Twain, 1894

In this chapter you will learn how to avoid online trading problems with your broker and how to solve problems should you encounter them. In spite of preventive measures, trading problems do occur. Some of these problems are legitimate bookkeeping errors that can be easily corrected, and others involve fraud and unlawful business practices conducted by con artists. By the end of this chapter you will know how to deal with the most common problems associated with online trading and where to go for assistance.

The saying, "an ounce of prevention is worth a pound of cure" is especially relevant when investing. The following are some of the most important preventative measures you can take as an investor.

Know Your Online Broker

Check with your state's securities regulator or the National Association of Securities Dealers (NASD) at 800-289-9999 for background information. Have they received complaints or has action been taken against either the broker (if you're using one for advice) or the broker's firm?

Is there a record of any complaints about this firm? Is the person recommending this investment licensed with your state securities agency?

Know Your Investment

- How does this investment match your investment objectives?
- How long has the company been in business?
- What are its products or services?
- Has the company made money for investors before?
- Is the investment registered with the SEC and the state where you live?
- Who is managing the investment? What experience do they have?
- Don't get swept away by a sales pitch.
- Ask for and carefully read the company's prospectus and latest quarterly or annual reports.
- Have a sales representative send you the latest reports that have been filed on a prospective investment.

Monitor Your Investments

Helpful Hint

Keep good records of all information you receive. Save copies of all forms you sign and statements of all purchases and sales transactions.

Examine carefully and promptly any written information of trades that you receive from your broker, as well as all periodic account statements. Make sure that each trade is completed in accordance with your instructions.

Check that the commission charged is in line with what you expected (a flat rate, percentage of transaction cost, or fee). If commission rates are to be increased, or if charges such as custodial fees are to be imposed, you should be informed in advance.

Know Your Rights

As an investor, you are protected by regulatory agencies that guarantee your right to be treated fairly and honestly by your broker and brokerage firm. In addition, you have recourse in the event of problems and disagreements. We will review these on a step by step basis, but first, here is a handy investor's guide to help you review your rights:

INVESTOR BILL OF RIGHTS
(Source: The American Association of Individual Investors)

1. Ask for and receive information from a firm about the work history and background of the person handling your account, as well as information about the firm itself.
2. Receive complete information about the risks, obligations, and costs of any investment before investing.
3. Receive recommendations consistent with your financial needs and investment objectives.
4. Receive a copy of all completed account forms and agreements.
5. Receive account statements that are accurate and understandable.
6. Understand the terms and conditions of transactions you undertake.
7. Access your funds in a timely manner and receive information about any restrictions or limitations on access.
8. Discuss account problems with the branch manager or compliance department of the firm and receive prompt attention to and fair consideration of your concerns.
9. Receive complete information about commissions, sales charges, maintenance or service charges, transaction or redemption fees, and penalties.
10. Contact your state securities agency in order to verify the employment and disciplinary history of a securities salesperson and the salesperson's firm; find out if the investment is permitted to be sold; or file a complaint.

Savvy Investor Tip

Many security fraud schemes are easily avoided once you recognize a characteristic that they all have in common: *this is too good to be true.* Whenever you hear yourself saying this to yourself, a gigantic alarm should go off in your head.

Real or Imaginary Gripe Against an Online Broker?

Before you work yourself into a frenzy about an error on your statement from your online broker, verify that the discrepancy isn't your fault. Backtrack all correspondence to find how, when, and if the error took place. Online trading is so quick and easy that novice traders frequently make trades they don't clearly recollect or understand. Spontaneous trades are often executed while caught up in the heat of the moment, especially when you feel an investment is hot or you overreact to market conditions. Impulsively executed transactions tend not to be recalled as easily as well-researched and planned trades.

This is why it is imperative that all online transactions be followed by a hard copy paper trail. All it takes is an inaccurate keystroke to change the entire nature of a trade. However, if you print out and save copies of all transactions and correspondences, discrepancies (whomever's fault they may be) can be easily verified and rectified.

CONTACT YOUR BROKER

If you are certain that you have a valid complaint against an online broker you have several resolution options. Most problems can be solved with a simple phone call or e-mail. Remember that securities brokers are under a tremendous amount of pressure from the SEC and the NASD to conform to existing laws and statutes. Severe penalties are imposed upon brokers who skirt the law. Most online brokers play by the rules and would much rather deal with complaints from customers quickly and directly without SEC or NASD intervention.

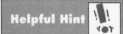 **Helpful Hint**

Legitimate brokers make their profit by commissions, not defending themselves against investigations and lawsuits from disgruntled customers, the SEC, or the NASD.

When solving problems with your online broker keep in mind that the simplest and least expensive solution is usually the best solution. Unless there is no doubt in your mind that a broker has committed a deliberate criminal act, it is best to adhere to the following list of grievance procedures step by step until the problem is resolved.

Following Through on Your Grievance with Your Broker

Before you contact your broker via e-mail or telephone, compose a written list of exactly what your grievance is and how you feel it should be resolved. Your documentation should include the times and dates that the problem transaction took place. It is also wise to fire up your computer and have your account information on screen before making the phone call to your broker. With complete documentation in front of you, you will not be distracted from your task. The person handling your complaint will immediately open your account on his or her computer and attempt to walk you through the problem. He or she will attempt to discover how the mistake took place. Listen carefully to his or her explanation and be open to the possibility that the problem is your fault, not your broker's.

By keeping the conversation friendly and upbeat you will be in a better position to receive helpful, professional advice on how to correct the problem. If you have not allowed much time to elapse before notifying the broker, the broker can usually correct the problem easily.

If the broker handling your account is not addressing the problem in the manner that you see fit, ask to speak with the manager of the brokerage. The manager most likely will the have experience and authority to correct most problems that occur with your online trading account.

If you feel like your complaint is not being properly resolved, proceed to the next level of conflict resolution, which is generally the firm's compliance department. You should put your complaint in writing and forward it to the firm's main office. State your complaint clearly and concisely. Tell them how you would like to see the problem rectified. Request the firm respond to you in within thirty days. If they do not respond in a satisfactory manner, it is probably time to make a formal complaint to the SEC or NASD.

How to Make a Complaint

The NASD and the SEC make it very easy to file a complaint against any person or entity connected to the securities market that you feel has defrauded you, especially if this occurred over the Internet.

Although these agencies instigate their own inquiries as they are warranted, they also rely heavily upon individual investors to come forth
with data. Your individual complaint may seem small to you, but it may
very well prevent another investor from losing his or her life savings.

Some of the most common complaints received by the SEC and the
NASD include:

1. failure of a business to register with the SEC
2. misrepresentation or omission of pertinent facts about a security
3. manipulation of market prices of securities
4. misappropriation of a customer's funds or securities
5. operation of a business while insolvent
6. buying or selling securities by a broker at unreasonable prices
7. using inside information to profit a broker or customer
8. wildly fluctuating stock prices for unknown reasons
9. unfair treatment of customers by brokers

The NASD *www.nasd.com* and the SEC *www.sec.com*. Web sites
have online complaint forms that are simple and convenient. Whether you
choose to file your complaint using the online form or a letter, you have
to supply the same essential information. The forms must be complete in
order for the SEC or NASD to complete their investigation of the matter.
You will need to include the following information:

1. The name of the brokerage firm and the individual broker whom
   you dealt with
2. The name of the security or securities in question
3. The behavior or practice that is the subject of the complaint
4. The dates and times of the alleged violation
5. Your name, address, and phone number

It is recommended that highly confidential information contained in
the complaint be personally transmitted via a phone call. Although the
investigation may lead to disciplinary action against the broker for regulatory infractions, it does not necessarily mean that you will receive complete monetary satisfaction. Another form of legal action may be
necessary to fully satisfy your claim.

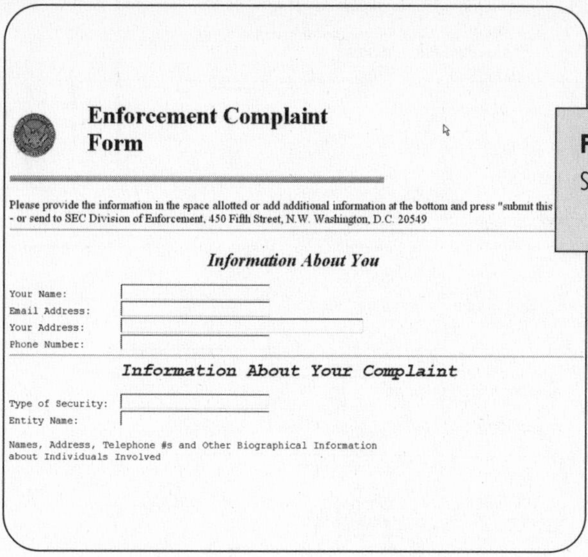

Enforcement Complaint Form

Please provide the information in the space allotted or add additional information at the bottom and press "submit this - or send to SEC Division of Enforcement, 450 Fifth Street, N.W. Washington, D.C. 20549

Information About You

Your Name:
Email Address:
Your Address:
Phone Number:

Information About Your Complaint

Type of Security:
Entity Name:

Names, Address, Telephone #s and Other Biographical Information about Individuals Involved

Figure 16-1

Screen shot of SEC Complaint form

ARBITRATION

Today, the use of arbitrators to resolve disputes between broker/dealers and their clients is the most common and accepted business practice. Most brokerage companies require new clients to sign a waiver the states that all disputes will be settled by arbitration rather than through the courts. Brokers prefer to settle disputes through arbitration because the cost is less and disputes are usually settled more swiftly. The same logic, generally, holds true for investors as well.

Arbitration hearings are conducted professionally, much like a court of law. Both parties may have their attorneys present. Both parties are expected to freely present evidence. After approximately thirty days both parties are provided with written notification of the arbitrator's decision.

An arbitrator's decision is based solely on the evidence provided. If you represent yourself, be sure to provide the arbitrators with sufficient evidence to find a judgment in your favor. Sponsoring organizations that provide the arbitrators have

FYI

Arbitrators are supposed to be impartial persons who understand the securities industry laws and practices. However, the arbitration panel does consist of people who are either employed or previously employed within the securities industry. This may create a built-in bias that does not favor investors.

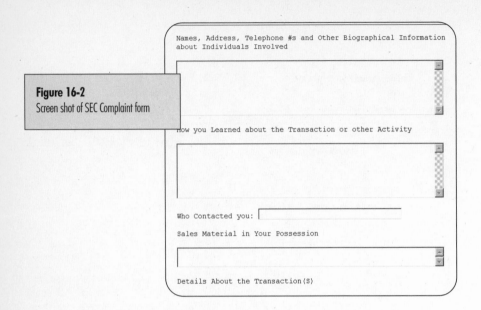

Names, Address, Telephone #s and Other Biographical Information
about Individuals Involved

How you Learned about the Transaction or other Activity

Who Contacted you:

Sales Material in Your Possession

Details About the Transaction(S)

Figure 16-2
Screen shot of SEC Complaint form

slightly different rules of order. Be sure to carefully read and understand the rules before entering an arbitration agreement. Arbitration agreements are legal and binding and should not be taken lightly.

MEDIATION

The mediation of disputes between brokers and their clients is another process to resolve complaints. It is less formal than arbitration or litigation in that the agreement reached between the parties is non-binding. The parties may drop out of the proceedings at any time and seek another form of action: litigation or arbitration. However, once a settlement is agreed upon and a contract is executed, the mediation agreement becomes a legal and binding contract. Mediation is usually less expensive than arbitration or litigation, but it is not without its costs, both monetary and psychological. The process can be slow and cumbersome but is far less draining than litigation.

LITIGATION

After all avenues of conflict resolution have been exhausted, litigation is sometimes necessary. The litigation process is usually reserved for cases where large monetary damages are claimed, usually a minimum of

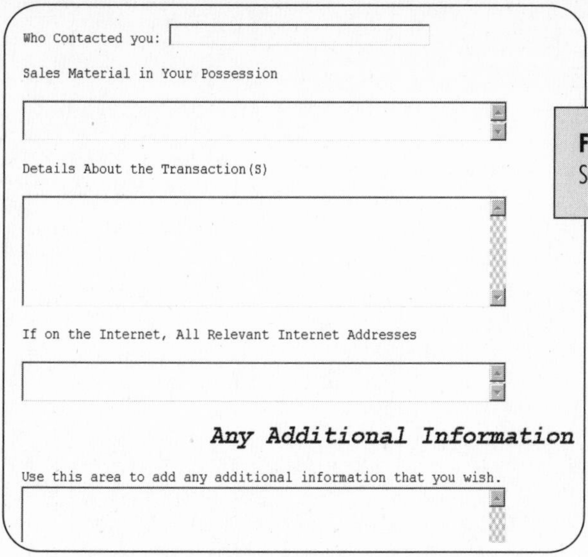

Who Contacted you: [_____]

Sales Material in Your Possession

[_____]

Details About the Transaction(S)

[_____]

If on the Internet, All Relevant Internet Addresses

[_____]

Any Additional Information

Use this area to add any additional information that you wish.

[_____]

Figure 16-3
Screen shot of SEC Complaint form

$10,000 dollars. However, the legal fees can easily exceed the monetary damages so proceed with caution when engaging the services of an attorney specializing in security law. In many cases, it is wiser to accept a smaller judgment offered out of court or through the mediation process than incur the risks and expenses of a drawn out legal battle.

Conclusion

After examining your options for recovering damages from a problem with your online broker, hopefully you will come to this conclusion: it is much less expensive and easier to take preventive measures than to recover damages. The Internet is a great hiding place for clever scam artists and that is not likely to change anytime soon. As soon as enforcement officials nab one crook, ten more appear in a new and more cunning disguise. Carefully follow the guidelines set forth in this book and you will less likely be a victim.

FYI

Most large brokerage houses maintain in-house attorneys who are able to devote extended periods of time to a case. For most individual investors, the legal costs associated with litigation are prohibitive. You might win the battle only to end up losing the war, financially speaking.

APPENDIX A

Glossary of Terms

American Depository Receipt A stock that is issued by an American bank, but backed by a foreign security that is held on deposit.

Annual Report A yearly report required of all publicly traded companies representing the current financial condition and outlook of coming year.

Annuity A contract with an insurance company which allows investments to accrue tax deferred, usually for retirement purposes and to avoid probate. Annuity contracts are either fixed or variable. Today, many variable annuity portfolios are managed by top mutual fund managers.

Arbitrage Simultaneously purchasing and selling equivalent securities or commodities with the intention of benefiting from a discrepancy in the price.

Arbitration This is a common way of settling legal disputes between parties in disagreement. Disputes are settled by an impartial board or individual. Investment related disputes are usually resolved in this manner.

Asking Price The lowest price a seller will accept for an investment.

Asset Allocation This is the breakdown of investments between cash, equities, fixed-income, and mutual funds. This should be done in relationship to your investor profile.

Basis Point This term is used to measure and quote yields on bonds, notes and t-bills. One basis point equals .01%, and 100 basis points equals 1%.

Bear Market A period of time, usually months or years, when stock prices generally decline.

Beta A method by which the risk of a particular investment is measured, usually stocks or mutual funds. This method compares the volatility of the investment against the volatility of the S&P 500. If the investment changes the same as the S&P it is said to have a beta of 1.00, or very little risk. If the investment changed 50% less than the S&P then it is said to have a beta of 0.50. The higher the beta the greater the risk.

Blue Chip A term to describe a large company that is a leader in its industry. Blue chip stocks are considered relatively safe investments. Blue chip refers to the largest denomination of gaming chips.

Bond A certificate which represents a loan. The issuer, who agrees to pay a set interest along with the principle when the bond matures, sets the terms.

Book Value The figure represented by subtracting a company's liabilities from its assets and then dividing it by the number of outstanding shares of common stock.

Breakpoint This term refers to the amount invested that results in a discount in sales charge in a mutual fund. The more you invest, the greater the discount.

Broker An intermediary between the buyer and the seller, commonly called a registered representative, account executive, or dealer. Brokers must be registered with the exchange where the securities are traded.

Bull Market A period of time, months or years, when stock prices rise.

Call An option to buy a commodity, security, or futures contract. The price is specified, as is the expiration date of the option contract.

Callable An issuer of a callable security has the right to redeem the issue when desired. This means you no longer own it but will get your money back.

Call Option This order entitles the buyer to purchase a set number of shares of a company at a set price for a specific length of time.

Capitalization This term refers to the sum total of a company's liabilities and equity. The ratio of debt to equity is computed by dividing the liabilities by the equity. The financial risk of an investment is very often determined by the debt to equity ratio.

Capital gain The difference between the purchase price and the sale price of an investment.

CBOE stands for Chicago Board of Options.

Certificate of Deposit A CD is a debt instrument issued by banks. Institutional CD's have denominations of $100,000 or more. Individual CD's may have value as low as $100. CD's pay interest and have preset maturity dates.

Churning This term describes the illegal practice of making multiple trades for a client with the intention of generating higher commissions.

Close The price of security at the end of a trading day.

Commission A fee charged by a broker for executing a trade. The amount of the fee is usually determined by the number of shares traded and/or the price of the trade. Online trading has lowered commission rates dramatically.

Common stock One share of stock in a company equals a share in ownership.

Cookie A code that a Web site on the Internet leaves on certain files in your harddrive, a kind of identification tag of you and your computer.

Corporate Bond This is a debt instrument issued by corporations to raise capital.

Convertible securities Securities in which the owner has the right to exchange for another security at a predetermined price for a set period of time.

Coupon rate This term refers to the interest rate a bond pays the investor.

Day Order This term refers to an order that is placed for execution during one trading session. It automatically expires if the trade isn't executed on that day.

Day Trading A speculative investment strategy which involves the buying and selling of securities in the same day.

Debenture This type of bond is issued without collateral. Debentures are paid after secured loans.

Dividend This is the payment of earnings to shareholders. Payment can be in money or stock. Dividends are usually paid quarterly.

Discount rate This is the interest rate that the United States Treasury charges banks. The Federal Reserve Board sets the rate, which strongly influences the nation's economy.

Dow Jones Industrial Average (DJIA) The average price of 30 actively traded blue chip stocks, consisting primarily of industrial stocks and a handful of service-oriented companies. This average can be a good barometer of the stock market. The DJIA is calculated by adding the closing prices of selected stocks and dividing them by the number of companies. The DJIA average is posted in points, not dollars.

Execution The completion of a trade by a registered broker.

Fiduciary A person authorized to make financial decisions and actions on behalf of another.

Fill or Kill This is an order to buy or sell a security. If the order isn't executed immediately it is invalid, or killed.

Fixed Income This term is often applied to government, corporate, municipal bonds, and preferred stock, all of which pay a fixed rate of interest.

Futures Contract An order in which the purchaser believes the price will go up for a security. Also, the seller speculates that the price will go down. This type of investment can be risky because more than the initial investment is at risk.

Good-till-Cancelled Order (GTC) An order to buy or sell a security at a particular price. It stays in effect until executed or canceled.

Hedging A strategy investors use to limit risk, much like betting both sides against the middle.

High This is the high price of a stock in daily trading. It can also describe the high price paid for a stock in the previous 52 weeks (one-year).

Indenture This document states the legal rights of the buyer and seller of bonds.

Individual Retirement Account (IRA) A personal, tax-deferred retirement account. Funds from this account may not be withdrawn prior to age 59½ without being subject to a tax penalty.

Immediate or Cancel Order An order requiring that all or part of the trade be executed as soon as it is received. If all or part of the trade is not executed it is canceled.

Insider A person who has non-public information about a company. It is highly illegal to use inside information.

Junk Bonds This describes bonds that have ratings below BBB by S&P, and below Baa by Moody's.

Keogh This refers to retirement plans for self-employed individuals.

Limit order An order which sets the buying or selling price of a security.

Listed Security This refers to securities that have been accepted by one of the registered securities exchanges in the United States. Listed securities include stocks, preferred stocks, bonds, convertible bonds, warrants, and options. Unlisted securities are traded in the Over-the-counter market (OTC).

Limit Price (Limit Order) This refers an order to buy or sell a security at a specific price or better.

Load Fund A mutual fund that is sold for a sales charge by a broker or representative who advises you when it is wise to buy or sell interest in the fund.

Low This refers to the lowest price paid for a security during a specific period, usually one day or a year.

Margin Account This describes a type of brokerage account which allows you to buy securities with funds loaned by the broker, by pledging the securities in your account as collateral.

Market Order This refers to a simple order that will be executed as soon as possible at the best available price. Market orders usually have the lowest commission cost.

M.I.T. (Market if Touched) This term refers to a price order which becomes a market order if a certain price is reached.

Markup A dollar amount that is added to the cost of securities purchased in the OTC market.

Markdown A dollar amount subtracted from the selling price of a security in the OTC market.

Money Market Fund This refers to funds that are invested in commercial paper, banker's acceptances, repurchase agreements, government securities, certificates of deposits, and other liquid assets that pay the going money market rate of interest.

Municipal Bond A debt obligation issued by the state or local government. The funds raised are frequently used for special public projects.

Mutual Fund A fund operated by an investment company that invests money from a pool of shareholders. The management is responsible for investing the money for a specific investment objective and adhering to its prospectus. Mutual funds offer the advantage of professional management.

NASDAQ National Association of Securities Dealers Automated Quotations System. The National Association of Securities Dealers

(NASD) controls this computerized system. It gives price quotations for securities traded over-the-counter as well as certain listed securities.

No-Load Mutual Fund A mutual fund offered by an open-end investment company that imposes no sales charge to its shareholders. No-Load does not mean no cost, however. Read your prospectus carefully. There's still no such thing as a free lunch.

Open Order A buy or sell order for securities that hasn't been filled, also called a good-till-canceled order.

Option This is a contract that gives the bearer a right but not the obligation to buy (call option) or sell (put option) a futures contract in a given commodity at a stated price. If the order isn't filled within a specified time it expires.

Order This term refers to the instructions an investor gives a broker when desiring to buy or sell a security. There are four basic categories for securities orders: market order, limit order, time order, and stop order.

Over-the-Counter Market (OTC) Consists primarily of unlisted securities that are not traded on one of the organized exchanges, such as the NYSE. The OTC market is conducted via telephone and computer, rather than an exchange floor.

Penny Stock Very low priced stocks that trade Over-the-Counter.

Pink Sheets Publication printed on pink paper which provides quotes on penny stocks.

Prospectus This is a written offer to sell a security. It states the terms and objectives of the investment and provides the financial details of the company and its officers. You should always read a prospectus carefully before investing.

Portfolio An individual investor's combined holdings of stocks, bonds, commodities, real estate, or any other asset.

Principal This term defines the main party in a transaction, a buyer or a seller. A principal buys or sells for his or her own account.

Proxy A person with the legal right to cast a vote for another.

Quote The highest bid or lowest offer price presently available for a security.

Range Refers to the high and low price of a particular security for the day.

Record Date The date you must be recognized as the owner of a record in order to be entitled to receive a declared dividend.

Red Herring This document is also called the preliminary prospectus and is used in new offerings.

Regular Way Refers to the standard trade settlement date, which is the 3rd business day following the trade date.

SEC The Securities and Exchange Commission was created in 1934 by the Securities Exchange Act. The agency's responsibility is to promote public awareness of illegal securities dealings.

Shares The actual paper certificate that states your share of equity ownership in a corporation.

Stop Price An order to buy or sell a security at a specified price or better, but only after a stop price has been reached or exceeded.

Short Sale A trade in which you "borrow" a stock in order to deliver the securities, with the intent to buy it at lower price later.

Stock Split When a corporation increases the number of shares outstanding without increasing the shareholders, equity. A two for one split means you simply own twice as much stock at half the pre-split price which neither increases or decreases its value.

Stop Order A market order that is executed only when the price entered is either reached or passed.

Takeover When one company acquires another company, which often results in the loss of a job for the acquired company's management.

Tender Offer A nice way of saying "we'd like to buy all your shares back." The offer can be in cash or securities.

Tick This refers to a change in price, up or down.

Ticker Symbol Letters that distinguish a security for trading purposes on the consolidated tape.

Trade Date The date a trade is made.

Treasury Bonds Long-term debt agents in denominations of $1000 or larger, which mature in 10 years or more.

Underwriters Investment bankers who bring new issues of stock like IPO's to market.

Uptick Refers to a listed stock that is trading at a higher price than its previous sale.

Volatility A term that refers to a security or market that has a sharp rise or fall in a short time frame.

Volume The total number of shares of stock traded during a specific period, usually a day.

Watch List This is a list of companies that are being scrutinized by a bro-kerage firm or regulatory agency to spot irregularities or possible takeovers.

Yellow Sheets The quote list of corporate bonds used by bond brokers.

Yield The rate of return on a specific investment.

Yield to Call The rate a bond will yield if held until it is redeemed by its issuer.

Yield to Maturity The rate a bond will yield if it is held to maturity.

Zero-Minus Tick When a stock trades at a price less than its last price, but equal to its last different trade.

Zero-Plus Tick When a stock trades at the same price as its last sale, but at a higher price than its last different price.

Zombies Companies that continue to operate even though they are no longer financially viable. May possibly be insolvent or bankrupt but still in existence.

APPENDIX B

Online Reference Section

ASSET ALLOCATION SITES

These sites offer asset allocation capabilities that can assist you with how to allocate your money into different types of investments based upon your needs and objectives.

FinancCenter, *www.financenter.com*
SmartMoney, *www.smartmoney.com*
Vanguard, *www.vanguard.com*

BONDS

Although trading bonds online is not as easy as it could be, these sites do offer some valuable information and assistance to bond and fixed income investors.

Bonds On-line, *www.bondsonline.com*
Bradynet, *www.bradynet.com*
CNNfn Bond Center, *www.cnnfn.com/markets/bondcenter*
ConvertBond.com, *www.convertbond.com*
Investing In Bonds.com, *www.investinginbonds.com*

CALCULATORS

Never again will you have difficulty calculating how much money
you'll need to invest to meet your goals, whatever they may be.
These calculators will do the work for you. Whatever the financial question, one of these calulator sites will help you find the answer.

FinanCenter, *www.financenter.com*
Money.com, *www.money.com*
MSN MoneyCentral *www.moneycentral.com*
Quicken.com, *www.quicken.com*
SmartMoney, *www.smartmoney.com*

CHARTS

Some people are more visually oriented and seeing the highs and lows of
the market or your favorite stocks on a chart may make more sense to you.
If that's the case, click on these sites for great charts and other helpful
information as well.

Big Charts, *www.bigcharts.com*
Clearstation, *www.clearstation.com*
Prophet, *www.prophetdata.com*

DRIPs & DSPs Sites

DRIPs are direct reinvestment programs that you allow you to reinvest
shares directly with certain companies. Some companies offer DSPs, or
direct stock purchase plans, which allow you to buy stock directly from
them rather than a broker. These sites will lead you to where to go take
advantage of these programs.

DRIP Advisor, *www.dripadvisor.com*
NetStock Direct, *www.netstockdirect.com*
Stock1.com, *www.stock1.com*

ECONOMIC DATA

Understanding the economy and its relationship to the markets is essential to you as an investor. Find out what the economic trends are and learn to anticipate their effect on your portfolio by checking out these sites regularly.

Federal Reserve, *www.stls.frb.org/other/websites.html*
Yahoo!Finance, *www.finance.yahoo.com*

FINANCIAL PORTALS

Financial portals offer extensive online investment services and information. They are constantly expanding their horizons so their features and benefits change almost daily.

Cyberinvest, *www.cyberinvest.com*
E-trade, *www.etrade.com*
Invest-o-Rama, *www.investorama.com*
Motley Fool, *www.fool.com*
MSN MoneyCentral, *www.investor.msn.com*
Wall Street City, *www.wallstreetcity.com*
Yahoo!Finance, *www.finance.yahoo.com*

FUNDAMENTAL RESEARCH

This is the most commonly used form of market research and analysis. Most of these sites make doing your research both easy to access and understand.

BestCalls, *www.bestcalls.com*
Briefing.com, *www.briefing.com*
Hoover's On-Line, *www.hoovers.com*
Investools, *www.investools.com*
Merrill Lynch, *www.ml.com/direct/research.htm*
Multex Investor Network, *www.multexinvestor.com*
Wall Street Research Net, *www.wsrn.com*
Wit Capital, *www.witcapital.com*
Yahoo!Finance, *www.finance.yahoo.com*

GOVERNMENT ASSISTANCE

If you have a problem, need advice or information on virtually any invest-ment related matter, there's someone out there who can help you. These sites are public "watch-dogs" and offer assistance free of charge.

Council of Better Business Bureaus, *www.bbb.org*
Due Diligence Board, *www.insidetheweb.com*
Federal Trade Commission, *www.ftc.com*
NASD Regulation, Inc., *www.nasdr.com*
Securities and Exchange Commission, *www.sec.gov*
Edgar On-Line, *www.edgar-online.com*
National Assocation of Securities Dealers, *www.nasd.com*
Social Security On-Line, *www.ssa.gov*

INITIAL PUBLIC OFFERINGS

Tired of wishing you had bought that IPO years ago when you just *knew* it was going to be a homerun stock someday? Want to get in on the latest tech offerings before they soar beyond reach? These sites will take you there if you can afford the risk and don't mind the ride.

IPO Central, *www.hoover.ipo.*
IPO Monitor, *www.ipomonitor.com*
OpenIPO, *www.openipo.com*
IPO Maven, *www.IPOmaven.com*

INTERNATIONAL INVESTING

The U.S. is not the only place to invest. Although mutual funds provide expert management in this realm, these sites will help you get there on your own if you are so inclined.

ADR.com, *www.adr.com*
The Emerging Markets Companion, *www.emgmkts.com*
TheStreet.com, *www.thestreet.com*

INVESTMENT FRAUD ORGANIZATIONS

Beware of *scams.com* should be the heading here. If you encounter a problem or want to brush up further on your fraud detection skills, these sites will help you.

Fraud Defense Network, *www.fdn.com*
Internet Scambusters, *www.scambusters.com*
National Fraud Information Site, *www.fraud.org*

INVESTOR EDUCATION

Again, education is the key to success, and there's an abundance of help available on these sites. Some require membership fees, others are free. Use them.

Alliance for Investor Education, *www.investoreducation.org*
American Association of Individual Investors, *www.aaii.com*
Fidelity Investments, *www.fidelity.com*
Security & Exchange Commission Investor's Education, *www.sec.gov.com*
S&P's Personal Wealth, *www.personalwealth.com*

MUTUAL FUNDS

Everything you ever wanted to know about mutual funds is available on these sites: from fund families, performance, research, and prospectus, you name it, it's out there.

Brill's Mutual Funds Interactive, *www.fundsinteractive.com*
FundAlarm, *www.fundalarm.com*
IndexFunds.com, *www.indexfunds.com*
Morningstar, *www.morningstar.com*
Mutual Fund Education Alliance, *www.mfea.com*
Mutual Fund Magazine, *www.mfmag.com*

ONLINE BROKERAGES

The list of online brokerage sites is growing by the day. What services they provide and at what cost changes daily. You'll find various ratings of these companies in articles written in major financial publications such as *Forbes, Fortune, Worth,* etc. You might try pulling these articles from their online archives to assist you.

A.B Watley, *www.abwatley.com*
Accutrade, *www.accutrade.com*
Active Investor, *www.preftech.com*
A.G. Edwards, *www.agedwards.com*
American Express Financial Direct, *www.american.express.com*
Ameritrade, *www.ameritrade.com*
Atlantic Financial, *www.af.com*
BCL Online, *www.bclnet.com*
Bidwell, *www.bidwell.com*
Brown and Company, *www.brownco.com*
Bull and Bear, *www.bullbear.com*
Charles Schwab, *www.schwab.com*
Citicorp Investments, *www.citicorp.com*
CompuTel, *www.rapidtrade.com*
Datek Online, *www.datek.com*
Discover Brokerage Direct, *www.discoverbrokerage.com*
DLJ Direct, *www.dljdirect.com*
Dreyfus, *www.dreyfus.com*
E*Trade, *www.etrade.com*
Empire Financial, *www.lowfees.com*
FarSight Financial Services, *www.farsight.com*
Fidelity Investments, *www.fidelity.com*
Firstrade, *www.firstrade.com*
ForbesNet, *www.forbesnet.com*
Fleet Brokerage, *www.fleet.com*
Freedom Investments, *www.fredominvestments.com*
Freeman Welwood, *www.freemanwelwood.com*
GFN Investments, *www.gfn.com*
GRO Corporation, *www.grotrader.com*

Internet Trading, *www.internettrading.com*
Investex Securities Group, *www.investexpress.com*
InvesTrade, *www.investrade.com*
J.B. Oxford, *www.jboxford.com*
Linder Funds, *www.linderfunds.com*
Livetrade, *www.livetrade.com*
Lombard Institutional Brokerage, *www.lombard.com*
Main Street Market, *www.mainstmarket.com*
Merrill Lynch, *www.merrilllynch.com*
MB Trading, *www.mbtrading.com*
Mr. Stock, *www.mrstock.com*
Morgan Stanley, Dean Witter, Discover & Co., *www.discoverbrokerage.com*
Muriel Siebert & Co., Inc., *www.siebertnet.com*
J.P. Morgan, *www.jpmorgan.com*
National Discount Brokers, *www.ndb.com*
Newport Discount, *www.newport-discount.com*
Pacific Brokerage Services, *www.tradepbs.com*
Paine Webber, *www.painewebber.com*
PAWWS Financial Network, *www.pawws.com*
Peremel Online, *www.peremel.com*
Preferred Trade, *www.preftech.com*
Prudential Securities, *www.prusec.com*
Quick and Reilly, *www.quick-reilly.com*
SAI Advisors, Inc, *www.on-lineinvest.com*
Saloman Smith Barney, *www.smithbarney.com*
Schwab, *www.schwab.com*
Scottsdale Securities, *www.scottrade.com*
Siebert, Muriel, *www.msiebert.com*
Smith Barney, *www.smithbarney.com*
Stocks4Less, *www.stock4less.com*
Suretrade, *www.suretrade.com*
Thomas F. White, *www.tfwhite.com*
Trade4Less, *www.trade4less.com*
TradeOptions, *www.tradeoptions.com*
Tradestar Investments, *www.tradestar.com*

Tradewell Discount Investing, *www.trade-well.com*
Trading Direct, *www.tradingdirect.com*
TruTrade, *www.trutrade.com*
Wall Street Access, *www.wsaccess.com*
Wall Street Discount Corporation, *www.wsdc.com*
Wang Investments, *www.wangvest.com*
Waterhouse Securities, *www.waterhouse.com*
A.B. Watley, *www.abwatley.com*
Web Street Securities, *www.webstreet.com*
Wilshire Capital Management, *www.wilshirecm.com*
Wit Capital, *www.witcapital.com*
Wyse Securities, *www.wyse-sec.com*
York Securities, *www.tradingdirect.com*
Ziegler Thrift, *www.ziegler-thrift.com*

ONLINE NEWLETTERS

These are some of the better newletters out there. Check them out to see if they offer anything that might be useful to you.

Fidelity Investor Newsletter, *www.fidelity.com*
Holt Stock Report, *www.metro.turnpike.net/holt*
InvestorGuide Weekly, *www.investorguide.com/weekly.htm*
Kiplinger Online, *www.kiplinger.com*

PORTFOLIO MANAGEMENT TOOLS

These sites offer loads of information on portfolio management and tools to help you do it.

Stockpoint Portfolio Management, *www.stockpoint.com*
Thomson Investors Network, *www.thomsoninvest.com*
Yahoo!Finance, *www.finance.yahoo.com*

NEWS SERVICES

The financial news is available 24 hours a day. You no longer have to wait for the 6:00 P.M. news to find out what happened. Check out the hot news stories throughout the day.

ABC News.Com, *www.abcnews.go.com/sections/business*
Bloomberg.com, *www.bloomberg.com*
CBS Marketwatch, *www.cbs.marketwatch.com*
CNNfn, *www.cnnfn.com*
Dow Jones Interactive, *www.djinteractive.com*
The Street.com, *www.thestreet.com*
Wall Street City, *www.wallstreetcity.com*
Wall Street Journal, *www.wsj.com*

QUOTES

Stock quotes are available everywhere online, certainly on most online brokerage sites. Here are a few of the best for quick, easy quotes.

Quote.com, *www.quote.com*
SmartMoney, *www.smartmoney.com*
Valueline, *www.valueline.com*
Wall Street City, *www.wallstreetcity.com*
Yahoo!Finance, *www.finance.yahoo.com*

RESEARCH REPORTS

Research reports from industry analysts are one of the most important aspects of investment research you should get accustomed to reading. These sites provide great research material.

Hoover's Online, *www.hoover.com*
Merrill Lynch, *www.merrilllynch.com*
MSN MoneyCentral, *www.investor.msn.com*
Zacks Investment Research, *www.zacks.com*

RETIREMENT PLANNING

Do you know how much you'll need to retire? Are you on target? Use these sites to help you get there.

Fidelity Investments, *www.fidelity.com/toolbox*
Go Figure, *www.forbes.com/calc*
Kiplinger, *www.kiplinger.com*

Search Engines

These sites will help you find anything you're looking for. Dogpile will do a search of all the search engines for you collectively.

AltaVista, *www.altavista.com*
Direct Hit, *www.directhit.com*
Dogpile, *www.dogpile.com*
Infoseek, *www.infoseek.com*
Saavy Search, *www.saavysearch.com*
Yahoo, *www.yahoo.com*

Stock Screeners

Stock screeners will help you locate the types of stocks you're interested in investing in. Test these two out to see which one works best for you.

Wall Street Voice, *www.wsvoice.com*
Yahoo!Finance, *www.finance.yahoo.com*

Tax Planning

Need help with your taxes? Here are a few helpful sites that might take some of the stress out at tax time.

Kiplinger Tax Cut, *www.taxcut.com*
Roth IRA Website, *www.rothira.com*
Secure Tax, *www.irs.ustreas.gov*
The Tax Prophet, *www.taxprophet.com*
TurboTax TaxCenter, *www.turbotax.com*
U.S.Tax Code Online, *www.fourmilab.ch/ustax/ustax.html*

Suggested Reading

The Great Boom Ahead by Harry S. Dent
A great book that looks with wisdom and optimism at the huge potential and profits to be made in the world of expanding economies.

The Warren Buffet Way, by Robert G. Hagstrom, Jr.
One of the classics outlining the strategies behind one of the best investment minds ever.

Stocks for the Long Run, by Jeremy Siegal
A must read for anyone who thinks there is any other place to invest than quality growth stocks. Buy the best, hold them for the long haul and watch your money grow.

Common Stocks and Uncommon Profits, by Phillip Fisher
Another classic that comes highly recommended by many investment gurus, including Warren Buffet.

One Up On Wall Street, by Peter Lynch
This easy to read book offers a lot of great guidelines for investors and is written by a man who has made a name for himself as a top-stock picker.

Creating Affluence, by Deepak Chopra
This is not your typical investment book by any means. It will, however, help you to change your attitude about "wealth consciousness." This may very well help you in your success with creating more money in your life.

Index